Financial Crime Risks

Challenges, Management
& Compliance

The African perspective

Kunda Emmanuel Kalaba

ISBN-13: 978-1533187086
ISBN-10: 1533187088

Copyright © 2016 Kunda Emmanuel Kalaba

Publisher: Elijah Miti Consultancy Enterprise
Email: WriteABookNGrowRich@gmail.com
www.WriteABookNGrowRich.com/Publishing-Packages

Contents

Foreword

Kunda Kalaba is a professional with 25 years' experience in managing public and private sector Financial Crime Compliance (FCC), Anti-Money Laundering (AML), Counter-Terrorism Financing (CTF), Trade and Economic Sanctions, Anti-Bribery and Corruption (ABC), Customer Due Diligence (CDD), Know Your Customer (KYC), High Risk Clients such as Politically Exposed Persons (PEPs), Jurisdictions and Industries, Suspicious Activity Report Reports (SARs), Cash Transaction Reports (CTRs), Customer Transaction Surveillance, Monitoring and Periodic Reviews, Crime Intelligence Operations, Fraud and Corruption Prevention, Detection, Examination and Investigations, Security, Law Enforcement Agency Operations and Regulatory Compliance.

Currently serving on the World Advisory Council of the Association of Certified Fraud Examiners (ACFE) Kunda Kalaba is also a member of the African Task Force Organising Committee, Speaker and Presenter at International Conferences for Association of Certified Anti-Money Laundering Specialists (ACAMS), public and private sector organizations. Member of the Association of Certified Compliance Professionals in Africa (ACCPA). Once served as Chairperson, Anti-Bribery and Anti-Corruption Working Group and Chairperson of the Bankers Association of Zambia (BAZ) Fraud Prevention and Security Committee for two terms of two years each. He is a founder member of the Institute of Directors (IoD), Zambian Chapter. A University of Zambia (UNZA) graduate, Kunda is highly skilled and versatile Certified Fraud Examiner (CFE), Certified Anti-Money Laundering Specialist (CAMS) and Certified Anti-Bribery and Corruption (ABC) prevention and investigator. Kunda has vast and sound experience in Financial Crime Risk Deterrence, Prevention, Detection, Investigations, Security and Prosecutions. He worked in several Countries within Sub-Saharan Africa, Europe, Middle East, Asia Pacific and the Americas with the Law Enforcement Agency, the Developmental Organisation and International Financial Institutions – Commercial, Corporate and Investment Banks.

Preface

In July 2009, the Author earned and received an elite and prestigious Certified Anti-Money Laundering Specialist (CAMS) designation. Kunda Kalaba was the third Zambian to receive this widely recognized CAMS® credential by the Association of Certified Anti-Money Laundering Specialists® (ACAMS®), the world's leading organization of professionals in the Anti-Money Laundering (AML) field.

The CAMS (Certified Anti-Money Laundering Specialist) designation is awarded to professionals who successfully complete a rigorous examination demonstrating their aptitude and expertise, and broad based knowledge on the challenging topic of international anti-money laundering detection and enforcement.

The examination covers money laundering and terrorist financing methods, the best practices to stop these crimes, the key legislation in place worldwide, global AML standards and developing defences for financial institutions to stop terrorist financing and money laundering. ACAMS headquarters is in Miami, Florida, USA.

In February 2013, a Press release prepared in Austin, Texas in the USA went like this; "Kunda Emmanuel Kalaba (CAMS) Earns CFE Credential" - Austin, TX USA – 9 February 2013, The Association of Certified Fraud Examiners (ACFE), the world's largest anti-fraud organization and leading provider of anti-fraud training and education, is pleased to award Kunda Emmanuel Kalaba of Lusaka in the Republic of Zambia the globally preferred Certified Fraud Examiner (CFE) credential. In order to become a CFE, Kunda Kalaba has met a stringent set of criteria and passed a rigorous exam administered by the ACFE.

Kalaba has successfully met the ACFE's character, experience and education requirements for the CFE credential, and has demonstrated knowledge in four areas critical to the fight against fraud: Fraudulent Financial Transactions, Fraud Prevention and Deterrence, Legal Elements of Fraud and Fraud Investigation.

Kunda Kalaba joins the ranks of business and government professionals worldwide who have also earned the CFE certification. Kunda Kalaba is currently the Area Head - Financial Crime Risk Operations for Southern and East Africa, Country Head Financial Crime Risk for Zambia and Country Money Laundering Prevention Officer (CMLPO). He is based in Lusaka, Zambia.

Certified Fraud Examiners (CFEs) have the ability to: examine data and records to detect and trace fraudulent transactions; interview suspects to obtain information and confessions; write investigation reports; advise clients as to their findings; testify at trial; understand the law as it relates to fraud and fraud investigations; and identify the underlying factors that motivate individuals to commit fraud. CFEs on six continents have investigated more than 1 million suspected cases of civil and criminal fraud.

The ACFE is the world's largest anti-fraud

organization and premier provider of anti-fraud training and education. Together with nearly 100,000 members, the ACFE is reducing business fraud world-wide and inspiring public confidence in the integrity and objectivity within the profession. Identified as "the premier financial sleuthing organization" by The Wall Street Journal, the ACFE has captured national and international media attention. For more information about the ACFE visit ACFE.com.

Acknowledgement

All the important and memorable moments; places, faces, tendencies and characters: everything I have had to encounter, from both the professional and social perspective, looped in sweeping, concise narratives shall be shared in a series of books of which this is the first.

I do most sincerely hope that the books which may follow shall read like a well-balanced tale of all the pain, the anxieties, the sense of hopelessness and the enthusiasm amidst the many losses and limited gains.

Each of us is a mere wayfarer in the journey of life, like everyone else I am indebted to all the people I have had to meet along the way, people whose input has had a bearing, good or bad, on my progress as a person and professional.

Above all else is the debt of gratitude I owe to certain persons whose love, understanding, empathy and encouraging attitude no amount or manner of citation can repay.

My Parents Marianna-Roberts and Peter-Dominic Kalaba, my dearest wife Rhudiah (RCK1), My lovely daughters - Kunda, Saffie, Katuta, Wangu; my Sisters Veronica, Julien, Juliet, Pauline, my brother Peter, all kith and kin whose support and belief in me have greatly helped during the first half century of my life.

I owe you an incalculable debt of gratitude. Thanks are in no small measure to my mentors and life Coaches for all your guidance and encouragement.

Introduction

Purpose To Write This Book

Professional Inspectors, Examiners and Investigators from both the Public Sectors such as Regulatory Bodies, Law Enforcement Agencies, Commissions and Authorities as well as those in Private Sector such as Banking and Financial Institutions including Security Firms face Financial Crime Risk challenges in their day today management, compliance and execution of various assignments.

Such professionals are frequently called upon and expected to handle investigation assignments in an impartial, effective and efficient manner which are all important both for the integrity of the profession and their reputations.

An investigators' code of ethics (COE) and Code of Conducts (COC) are good starting points in any industry, but they only outline expectations. Investigators need the deep knowledge, technical skills and broad experience to anticipate and react when an ethical issue arises during the process and procedures of conducting investigations with a human and professional face.

Those who have been close to the Financial Crime Scenes and Action know that the amounts of money involved could be enormous. The various crimes which generate colossal sums of this money could be very unpleasant.

The Human beings who commit these heinous criminal activities can be unpleasant, uncompromising, hard-hearted and mostly very dangerous.

Lest we forget, their wealth and connections mean that they are often more powerful and influential and would crave to go into African Politics in order to become "untouchables", immuned, insulated and protected by the "honourable" worldly titles.

In this book, I will endeavour to share some of the professional experiences without risking the breach of oath of secrecy, examine some of the most pressing ethical issues investigators face in the fervent belief and hope that Institutions will provide their own practical strategies for navigating these murky ethical waters safely from the African perspective. Some of the salient points which may be considered after having read this book are;

a) What are the most common ethical issues, professional dilemmas and quandaries faced by investigators? What Lessons to learn from real life-like case scenarios presented

b) What are some of the factors to consider in the decision on who to assign to head Compliance Department, conduct a complex and high profile investigation case internally and externally.

c) How to professionally handle Regulatory Compliance, effective coordination and liaison with Law Enforcement Agencies, Knowing Your Employees and Knowing Your Customers.

d) What is the critical role of the Board of Directors, Senior Executive Management and Staff in the fight against financial crimes?

Working Definitions

Corruption is the dishonest, illegal, immoral behavior, fraudulent conduct involving bribery, abuse of office for private gain by officials in the public and private sectors, in which they improperly and unlawfully enrich themselves and those close to them, by misusing the position in which they are placed.

Fraud is any intentional or deliberate act or omission designed to deceive others, resulting in the victim suffering a loss and/or the perpetrator achieving a gain. Fraud is said to have been committed when a person causes a loss or potential loss to another by making a false representation with intent to deceive.

Money Laundering (ML) is the process by which criminals attempt to conceal or disguise the ownership and origin of the proceeds of criminal activity so that the funds *appear* to be derived from legal sources. ML process does not make the funds legitimate or become clean, it just makes them appear to be legitimate or clean. It still remains dirty money.

Terrorist Financing (TF) is an act of any person where by any means, directly or indirectly, unlawfully and willfully, provides or collect funds with an intention that they be used, or in the knowledge that they are to be used, in part or in full, to sponsor or facilitate a terrorist activity or act.

Customer Due Diligence (CDD) is a process where Financial Institutions such as Banks, Insurance Companies, Securities and Broking firms collect, maintain, periodically review and update information and data about their individual clients, corporate, commercial and Institutional customers. Customer Due Diligence (CDD) process is a Legal and Regulatory requirement to allow an informed choice to be made whether to onboard a new customer, continue with an existing customer relationship, or provide a new product or service or in worst case scenario, deny/reject the service and exit the relationship and close the Client's or Bank account. It is also one of the most powerful and available tools at the banks disposal to prevent and deter financial criminals and terrorist financiers from using the banks as conduits to conduct their illegal activities.

Chapter One

Devastating Impact of Financial Crime

Three contractors in the Civil Engineering field in Zambia were bidding to mend the pot-holed and re-construct a five hundred kilometers stretch of road which also meant building several bridges and drainages all the way from Lusaka to Livingstone Town. They meet with some Government officials from several responsible Ministries and Agencies to draw up their quotes.

The first contractor, a Zambian of Indian origin takes out a file, does some paperwork based on previous experience. He then punches some figures into his scientiflc Casio calculator and eventually tells the officials that the job would cost ZMW900million (mobilisation and material K400m, labour K400m and K100m profit).

The second contractor, who is a Chinese national married to an indigenous Zambian lady, does the same and said he could do the job for ZMW700million (material K300m, labour K300m and K100m profit).

The third person runs a business in Kabwe Town, Central Province as a Food and Stationery Supplier Shop. He is actually an indigenous, native and local Zambian. He doesn't measure or use his calculator but whispers to Government Officials and tells them ZMW2.7billion. The Government Civil Service officials wondered and said to the Zambian masquerading as a contractor; "You don't have necessary earth moving equipment, you didn't even do any calculations, and how did you come up with such a high figure"? The man replied; "ZMW1billion for me, ZMW1billion for you and ZMW700million to hire the Chinese national and his company to do the job".

This sad story of "Tenderprenueres" has been told by many to illustrate how and why corruption in most developing Countries is said to be endemic and rampant. Corruption as we all know can lead to massive waste and in the uneven allocation of scarce national resources. Does this sound familiar?

There is a paper entitled "The Devastating impact of Money Laundering and other Economic and Financial Crimes on the Economy of Developing Countries: Nigeria as a Case Study by Yusuf and Ibrahim from the International Islamic University Malaysia"

The paper makes very interesting reading. You are encouraged to read, if you have a moment to spare. You can Google it up online and may just open up our minds to digest situations in our Countries.

The paper argues that Economic and financial crimes represent a dangerous form of criminal behaviour that affects not only individual member of a society but also having deleterious effects on the economic, health and material welfare of the community as a whole.

Economic and financial crimes are non-violent criminal practices which are tantamount to sabotage of the national economy. This is because of the impact of these offences on the social well-being and economic foundation of any nation.

This paper examines the general consequences of

economic and financial crimes especially money laundering on the economy of the developing countries using Nigeria as a case study. The study finds that the common characteristic of the effects of economic and financial crimes in the developing countries is its tendency to undermine a nation economy which in turn often results in decelerated improvement in the quality of life of citizens and paving way for economic cum political stagnation.

This finding represents a major problem Nigeria like many other developing countries is presently grappling with as a result of the prevalence of economic and financial crimes. The paper concludes by recommending a strong legal regime coupled with political will to combat the menace and minimise its devastating consequences.

In Section three (3) subsection one (1), on the consequences of economic and financial crimes in Nigeria, some very alarming figures are mentioned. The gloomy picture reminds us of Zambia and our God Given Natural and Mineral Resources notably among many - "Copper".

The paper states, "In spite of Nigeria's enormous oil and gas deposit and abundant human resources, the nation is still a poor country with 80-90 million Nigerians out of the 140 million population living in abject poverty.

For the past four decades, over USD300 billion was earned from oil exports but paradoxically Nigeria's current per capital income is about 20% less than the 1975 level while the nation suffers under an excruciating external debt burden of about USD33 Billion, equivalent of 60% of the nation's GDP.

The pathetic consequences of economic and financial crimes in Nigeria is well captured by Nuhu Ribadu, the former Executive Chairman of the Economic and Financial

Crimes Commission (EFCC) Nigeria, when he disclosed thus; " Without seeking to befog you with statistics, let me share a few example of what corruption has cost us as a people and as a nation. My pet example is the GDP20 Billion Pounds (about USD500 Billion) of development assistance that has been stolen from this country since independence to date by past leaders of our country ...the money could create the beauty and glory of Western Europe six times all over Nigeria.

Nigerians line up at the gate of Western Embassies daily in search of visas to flee the country, but the best way to appreciate this figure is to recall that it represents six times the value in money that went into rebuilding Europe via the famous Marshal at the end of the 2nd World War.

We need to seriously introspect, reflect on the current and future state of the many Countries on the African Continent.

Chapter Two

Genesis of Career, Path and Foundation

By the time I was graduating on 15th December 1990 at Mulungushi Conference Centre in Lusaka, Zambia and Dr. Kenneth David Kaunda as the last Republican Presidential Chancellor of the University of Zambia, I was faced with three opportunities to serve the Nation.

The first one was to serve under the Department of Elections under Cabinet Office. This Department was later transformed into a present day Electoral Commission of Zambia (ECZ).

The second option was to go and teach English Language, Literature in English and Geography at St, Clement's Secondary School in Mansa. This Catholic Missionary School had already a partially furnished house which included stove, curtains, bed and mattress, furniture and all what a fresh graduate, single handsome bachelor would yearn for. This is the same School I had attended during my Secondary School Education from Form one to Form five from 1981 to 1985. I had no excuse. I knew the school and the good environment around Mansa very well. I had spent almost 7 years of my life in this town and I knew it well to go round and survive..

The third option was to join the Anti-Corruption Commission, another Government of the Republic of

Zambia Institution. Although the three were public Institutions run by Government of the Republic of Zambia, the gross salary structures and accompanying conditions of service were very different and far wide apart.

It was the first test in real life decision making, risk taking considerations and looking at the bigger picture at that younger age. The concept theory of Strengths, Weaknesses, Opportunities and Threats (SWOT) Analysis had just been introduced in Zambia and not very well understood or greatly appreciated by so many people. For reasons some of my close friends and relatives will never ever understand, I opted to work for the Anti-Corruption Commission to be based in Lusaka. With no accommodation guaranteed for the next four years, some of my Colleagues have always told me in the face, that it may not have been the wisest decisions I have ever made. I have no personal regrets and I have never looked back ever since.

I worked from 1st January 1991 to 1st January 2000 at Anti-Corruption Commission (ACC). Senior Corruption Prevention and Investigations Manager was my last known title. After an intense 3 month Induction Training Course, my first appointment then was Assistant Investigations Officer. From 1991 to 1995, I worked in the Republican Presidential Inquiries Unit and promoted to the Head of Corruption Prevention Department. The Commission Offices were located at Plot number 25 Independence Avenue, Kamwala and 18th Floor at Findeco House.

Just to delve back in history. The legal provisions that outlawed corruption in independent Zambia were first contained in the penal code, CAP 146, Chapter X of the laws of Zambia. This legislation was exclusively concerned with corruption offences by persons employed in the public sector but did not take offence with corruption transactions by or with private bodies or agents.

It was therefore deemed to be inadequate in as far as fighting corruption is concerned. The Zambia Police Force then now Zambia Police Service (ZPS) which was charged with the duty of enforcement was also not able to adequately deal with corruption offences. In 1980, a bill in parliament was passed that culminated into the establishment of the Anti-Corruption Commission that was going to exclusively deal with corruption cases.

The Anti-Corruption Commission (ACC) is the Agency that is mandated to spearhead the fight against Corruption in Zambia. It was established in 1980 under an Act of Parliament, the Corrupt Practices Act No. 14.

The background of the Anti-Corruption Commission lies in these efforts to fight this scourge of corruption. The Commission is mandated to spearhead a broad Anti-Corruption Mandate of investigation, prosecution, prevention and public education. This mandate anchors the Commissions core functions of enforcement, prevention, education which are a pillar of its existence. We fondly called this "the three pronged attack" on corruption.

The Anti-Corruption Commission is mandated to prevent and take necessary and effective measures for the prevention of corruption in public and private bodies.

The Commission receives and investigates complaints or cases of alleged or suspected corrupt practices, and subject to the directions of the Director of Public Prosecutions, prosecute those suspected of involvement in corruption. Investigating any conduct of any public officer which in the opinion of the Commission may be connected with or conducive to corrupt practices.

These approaches sometimes require joint efforts with other Law enforcement Agencies like in the case of the Task Force on Corruption, Zambia Police Service, Drug Enforcement Commission and several other Security

23

Services. The ACC also disseminate information on the socio-economic effects of corrupt practices, and enlist and foster public support against corrupt practices; and, do such things as are incidental or conducive to the attainment of the functions.

Under the Community Education, the ACC has developed deliberate policy of inculcating a culture of zero-tolerance for corruption among the youth through youth festivals, school anti-corruption clubs and school curriculum. Together, various ways including partnering with the private sector, civil society, artists and the general public are adopted to achieve the goal. The three pronged approach and attack on Corruption resembles many jurisdictions especially around the African Region. I had the privilege of working and supporting all the three divisions.

Let us drill down to what exactly is corruption. Several interest groups may understand this scourge differently. Admittedly, there are many definitions.

Last time I checked the Longman Contemporary English Dictionary defines corruption as 'the dishonest, illegal, or immoral behaviour, especially from someone with power'.

The Oxford Dictionary though says corruption is the dishonest or fraudulent conduct by those in power, typically involving bribery.

The World Bank defines corruption as 'the abuse of public office for private gain', yet the Asian Development Bank has shared that "Corruption involves behaviour on the part of officials in the public and private sectors, in which they improperly and unlawfully enrich themselves and/or those close to them, or induce others to do so, by misusing the position in which they are placed."

Transparency International says, "Corruption involves behaviour on the part of officials in the public sector, whether politicians or civil servants, in which they improperly and unlawfully enrich themselves, or those close to them, by the misuse of the public power entrusted to them."

The Swedish International Development Agency (SIDA) defines corruption as 'when institutions, organizations, companies or individuals profit inappropriately from their position in the operations and thereby cause damage or loss. This includes giving and receiving bribes, extortion, favoritism and nepotism, embezzlement, fraud, conflict of interest, and illegal monetary contributions to political parties.'

Several international conventions and protocols like the United Nations Convention against Corruption, the African Union (AU) Convention on the Prevention and Combating of Corruption and the Southern African Development Community (SADC) have provided definitions of corruption.

In Zambia, the current law that addresses corruption is the Anti-Corruption Act No. 3 of 2012. The law defines corruption as the "The soliciting, Accepting, Obtaining, Giving, Promising, and Offering of a gratification by way of a bribe or other personal temptation or inducement".

We note that the new Law has brought back the "misuse or abuse of public office for private gain or benefit" and has continued with the "possession of unexplained property" which may have been removed before the 2011 General Elections. We would not like to follow that path or wish to tabulate the reasoning for or against these clauses. We all recall that Professor Patrick Mvunga SC strongly argued his professional legal views on these issues.

The latter aspect of unexplained property entails that being in control of pecuniary resources whether cash under the pillow, cash buried underground on the farm, many vehicles and bicycles in the garage, money in the local and offshore Bank accounts, luxury yachts, boat houses and cruise ships and property like dwelling, residential or commercial building, small holding or farm, or maintaining a standard of living above that which is commensurate with the public officer's present or past official emoluments or other income would constitute corruption.

As Zambians, regardless of the fact that we are still largely a cash economy, we need to learn the art and science of being transparent, accountable by keeping records of income and expenditure, keep the pay slips, salaries, wages, allowances, bonuses and gratuity, business transactions, tax invoices and receipts.

The law allows the ACC Officers to summon anyone who is alleged to be in receipt of benefits of any service which the public officer may reasonably be suspected of having received corruptly or in circumstances which amount to an offence under the Anti-Corruption Act.

Unless we are all above board - the contrary is proved, the public officer will be liable for the offence having under his/her control resources or property reasonably suspected of having been corruptly acquired or having misused or abused his office.

We leave it there. We do not wish to go into Legal issues of why the "burden of proof" and proving innocent has been placed squarely on the shoulders of a suspect rather than "he who alleges must prove". That is for your Attorney to atone for your alleged sins and breaches.

We also note that under the said ACC Act, a 'gratification' is defined as 'any corrupt payment, in cash or "in kind". Other than a 'casual gift', gratification includes:

(a) Money, any gift, loan, fee, reward, commission, valuable security, property, or interest in property of any description, whether movable or immovable.

(b) Any employment or contract of employment or services and any promise to give employment or render services in any capacity;

(c) Any payment, release, discharge or liquidation of

any loan, obligation or other liability, whether in whole or in part;

(d) Any service, favour or advantage of any description, such as protection from any penalty or from any action or proceedings of a disciplinary or penal nature, and including the exercise or the omission from the exercise of any right of any official power or duty;

(e) Any valuable consideration or benefit of any kind, discount, commission, rebate, bonus deduction or percentage;

(f) Any right or privilege; and

(g) Any aid, vote, consent or influence. Therefore any person, (public official or a private person) who by himself or in conjunction with another person solicits, accepts, obtains, gives, promises, or offers a gratification by way of a bribe or other personal temptation or inducement commits an offence.

Since ignorance is not a defence, especially for law enforcement and Investigations professionals tasked to execute financial crime assignments, we all need to know that a person shall therefore be guilty of an offence of corruption or abuse of authority of office under this Act if he/she directly or indirectly does the following:

1. Receives gratification as an inducement:

(a) To voting or abstaining from voting at any meeting in favour or against any matter.

(b) To performing or abstaining from performing,

hindering or preventing performance.

(c) To aid in procuring or preventing the passing of any vote or any contract or advantage in favour of any person.

(d) To give assistance or used to influence:

> i. the promotion, execution or procurement of any contract with a public or private body or any sub- contract to perform any work, provide any service or supply any article.

> ii. The payment of the price, consideration or other moneys stipulated in any such contract or sub-contract.

(e) To withdraw a tender or the refraining from the making of a tender for any contract with a public or private body.

(f) On account of gaining from bidding at any sale auction conducted by or on behalf of any public or private body.

(g) On account of refraining or having refrained from bidding at any auction conducted by or on behalf of any public or private body.

2. Any person who being a public officer has abused his/her office to obtain property, wealth, advantage or profit or maintains a standard of himself/herself above his/her present or past official emoluments or is in control of pecuniary resources disproportionate to his present or past official emoluments or is in receipt of the benefit of any services which he/she may reasonably be suspected of having received corruptly.

The first part of the definition of corruption in the Act clearly states the conditions under which corruption can be said to have taken place.

These are:

I.   Asking or soliciting for a gratification.

II. Accepting

III. Obtaining

IV. Giving

V.   Promising; and

VI. Offering of a gratification.

Each of these above instances therefore constitutes an offence of corruption.

Just to be pretty sure, this definition of corruption encompasses both public and private persons. More Interesting is the fact that even if no money or any other form of payment has been made, the sole act of promising, offering, or soliciting is an offence.

Private citizens, individual in the Private Sector like those in Banking and Finance, Insurance and Broking, Securities and Exchange, Money Services Business and a whole lot of other Industries who attempts to bribe or is offered a bribe by another private person, the mere act of offering a bribe and you accept, you have both committed an offence under the Anti-Corruption Act. Under this Law, both the giver and the receiver can be charged.

An interesting example of this sort of corruption is the exchange of sexual favours for preferential treatment, promotion, or employment, endorsement, nomination or election. I have handled several cases where a superior, boss, manager or senior official demanding sex from his or her subordinate in exchange for promotion, bonus, salary increment or to drop a civil, criminal or disciplinary cases. This is a dangerous career limiting path to embark on.

Our advice is that anyone demanding for such a sinful and adulterous favour must be reported to the ACC and they would carry a serious "Surveillance operation on the "Cheaters" and culprits will or can be prosecuted. So says the law.

College and University Lecturers are warned. Demanding sex from a student in exchange for very good or better grades is an offence. The same law applies to students who offer sex to teachers, lecturers in exchange for better grades when one does not deserve those high marks. Simply study hard. Be honest. Graduate with "A"s and not with AIDS. Rewards are enormous and your reputation and integrity will vouch for you in real working life.

Chapter Three

Lesson Learnt From
Dr. Kenneth David Kaunda

I specifically enjoyed making appointments with State House and securing appointments for my boss and I to meet His Excellency, the Republic President – Dr. Kenneth David Kaunda and late Mr. President - Dr. Frederick Titus Jacob Chiluba and informing them which of the Senior Officials were not abiding to the Leadership Code then under Dr. Kaunda and those in leadership who fell below the new democratic dispensation under Dr. Frederick Chiluba. The first Cabinet Ministerial reshuffles and casualties under Dr. FTJ Chiluba was a result of the several assignments executed by our Department.

In my early career, I vividly recall one day when my boss and I were in State House (famous Plot 1) giving our usual bi-weekly briefing, Dr. K.D. Kaunda over one case where we were updating him on the searches we had carried out at one of his own inner cycle Senior Officials.

His Excellence, instructed us to wait for about fifteen minutes whilst he stepped out of his "Oval Office". As he walked out of his Office, my mind wondered how not long ago, we as University of Zambia (UNZA) students had denounced the President and petitioned him at the same state house grounds less than a year earlier.

My thoughts took me to the day when the same man was conferring a degree on me as our Chancellor and here I was seated in his Office waiting for him whilst gazing at amazing great piece of artwork in his Office. My mind kept on wondering whether his "system" and Closed Circuit Television (CCTV) cameras had picked me as one of those "naughty" University of Zambia (UNZA) students chanting unpalatable mob-psychology induced anti-government "Vivas" in the streets of Lusaka a year earlier.

When he emerged, Dr. Kaunda personally gave me two letters stamped "State House" to be delivered to the Chief Executive Officer and Managing Director of one of the big Parastatal Companies under the ZIMCO Group of Companies then. Little did I know that one white envelop contained an "appointment" or "promotion" letter and another brown envelop contained a "disappointment" letter which was actually an "instant summary dismissal" for the said Chief Executive Officer and Managing Director.

One important lesson I learnt from that unfortunate incident was that sheer greediness, blatant dishonesty and corrupt tendencies can bring up untold misery, ruin your life permanently and send you to an early grave. Sadly, the said Chief Executive Officer had marital problems after the letter of dismissal which I personally delivered to his Office and handed over to him within his very posh and spacious Office. The girlfriend abandoned him, friends became few and scarce, some relatives shunned and abandoned him, he suffered from shame and discontinued playing golf, When the new Government of the Movement for Multi-Party Democracy (MMD) could not honour their promise of giving him a big post within the Government circles after examination of the Anti-Corruption Commission report my boss and I had jointly compiled, the MD/CEO died of depression.

I played a role in the recruiting, training, coaching and mentoring staff in corruption prevention and investigations departments to my colleagues who joined the Commission in later years. On the investigations side, I was privileged to be part of the professional team members to investigate high profile cases such as Chief Executive Officers, Ministers, and other Senior Government Officials.

We used to examine the practices and procedures of client organizations and facilitating the discovery of corrupt activities and all forms of malpractices throughout the Country. Under the Corruption Prevention of which I later became the Departmental Head, we used to give professional advice to organizations and institutions on ways and means of promoting accountability, transparency, reducing and preventing opportunities for corruption and fraud.

From 1995 to 2000 I designed, co-coordinated, facilitated, implemented, monitored and evaluated USAID, DFID, NORAD, SIDA, CIDA, JICA, DANIDA and FINISH funded projects of "Managerial Accountability Workshop Account"- MAWA.

Whilst working for the Commission, I was the Team Leader assigned to work with Zambia Revenue Authority (ZRA) to revamp the revenue collection. I was appointed Commissioner to review the National level examination malpractices (leakages) at Examination Council of Zambia (ECZ). We toured Provincial Capitals and gathered evidence and proposed measures to curb the scourge.

I was privileged to lead a team on a covert operation at Zambia Electricity Supply Corporation (ZESCO) on clandestine and surveillance operations and arrested Senior Managers, Officers and handymen who received bribes from customers for having illegally installed electricity poles and supplied power to unreticulated shanty compounds such as Chazanga, Chipata overspill and Mandevu which was never approved.

I was more or less like a Government to Government Consultant and was part of the team who supported and spearheaded the establishment of the Anti-Corruption Bureaus and Commissions against Corruption and Economic Crimes in Southern African Development Community (SADC) and Common Market for Eastern and Southern Africa (COMESA) Countries.

I was part of the working Committee member who formulated and implemented the establishment of the Institute of Directors (IoD) Zambia chapter and by that token, I consider myself as an Honorary and life Founder member of IoD.

I led a Team which studied the wanton exploitation and destruction of forest resources in Eastern, Western, Copperbelt and Southern Provinces. I had written a project proposal and obtained the financial support from World Wide Fund (WWF) for Nature, Malawi Office.

It was during my stint at Anti-Corruption Commission where I was given an opportunity to travel to almost all the Provinces of Zambia and to so many Towns and Districts on various National assignments.

Between January 1990 and December 1999, I met most of the Cabinet Ministers, Deputy and Provincial Ministers and the Permanent Secretaries and their Directors under Dr. Kenneth Kaunda and Dr. Frederick Titus Jacob Chiluba in my Official capacity to resolve matters of national interest.

At a very young age, the Republic of Zambia had conferred upon me the rare privilege of picking up a phone and directly call any Managing Director or Chief Executive Officer of both the Private and Public Institution and secure an appointment to meet either in their Office, my Office and any other convenient hotel for a "friendly discussion".

After all, an attested Officer like me during those days of the State of emergence had power and authority to detain any Zambian in the Police Cells anywhere within the Republic of Zambian Boundaries without formally charging them. Human Rights Commission did not exist at that time. We used the authority responsibly though respecting all human beings.

We were the first occupants of the Kajeema flats behind the Chilenje main bus station near the market. Michael Chilufya Sata as a Minister of Local Government and Housing under Dr. FTJ. Chiluba had embarked on that housing project of demolishing old grass thatched houses and replaced them with those flats and houses which were initially given to Zambia Army Officers, Zambia National service Officers, Zambia Air force and other Security Wings among them the Anti-Corruption Commission. We had shared a two bed-roomed flat with my late colleague Milton Malunga Lunga for more than five years. Milton only moved out of Chilenge flat to stay in Woodlands when he got promoted and married leaving me behind the Kajeema Flat number four (4), Block One (1).

The second Zambian Republican President Frederick Jacob Titus Chiluba came up with a Housing Policy to sell Government, Ministries, Agencies, Councils, Mining, Institutional Houses and Commission Houses to sitting tenants. I applied to buy the Kajeema flat where I had stayed for eight years.

When the Office of Secretary to the Commission refused to grant permission for my colleagues and I to buy those Kajeema flats as first sitting tenants claiming they were "Transit homes" for Officers, most of us were shocked. Unfortunately for us, we could neither protest nor go on strike without the risk of being arrested under "mutiny" clause of the law of the land. We could not agree on the new definition of "transit" as eight years was too long for anyone of us to have been in "transit" in the same small flat.

To make matters worse, most of us were already married. I had two daughters by September 1999. To add salt to the accommodation injuries, when I was promoted to Senior Investigations manager or Officer, the Housing Committee of the Ministry of Works and Supply had allocated me a Government house in Olympia Extension, number 6 Akataka road within Lusaka.

Unknown to me one of the Senior Line Managers was eyeing the same house despite the fact that she was already married to a Government Official and as a Couple working in Government, they had been collectively and jointly allocated a very big house in Olympia Park.

There were no Government House loans which could let me afford to obtain a house mortgage loan during those days. Zambia National Building Society and Pan African Building Society would ask for collateral which none of us working in Government or Commission had at that time. I honestly loved my job, performed well, as the performance appraisals were very good in terms of execution of the national assignments.

Many things about us are true because we tell ourselves they are true. Many aspects of the way we live and act, think and view the world can change by simply changing the stories we should tell ourselves about ourselves.

People deserve a life that is full and rich. We must envision the story of that life, and start repeating it ourselves even if when we are taking that cold shower during the coldest month of the year. The way we respond to life is a function of the way we see ourselves responding to life and the heavy punches the World throw at us.

The way we move through each day is deeply affected by the way we imagine ourselves doing so. As these thoughts ran through my mind, I started looking for other opportunities to make those stories more positive and empowering.

Develop an attitude of gratitude, and give thanks for everything that happens to you, knowing that every step forward is a step toward achieving something bigger and better than your current situation. **Brian Tracy's words were ringing a bell in my head.**

We cannot change our past. We cannot change the fact that people act in a certain way. We cannot change the inevitable. The only thing we can do is play on the one string we have, and that is our attitude. - **Charles R. Swindoll**

Sometimes, things happen to us we can't comprehend. We hurt, we cry and we experience pain that pinches and bites our heart and makes us cold. But the best thing is that it always gets better and better; it's just about appreciating the good times more than the bad times.

There is little difference in people, but that little difference makes a big difference. The little difference is attitude. The big difference is whether it is positive or negative. - **W. Clement Stone**

You cannot stop life from changing, and you wouldn't really want to. Life by its very definition is a process of change. The only constant thing in anyone's life is change. Though you cannot stop life from changing, you can choose to successfully deal with the changes. In fact, you can learn, adapt and adjust in ways that change your own life for the better. Every time the world changes, new positive opportunities are born. And somewhere, in some way, the world is changing in every moment. Instead of wishing that things had stayed the same, I started looking for new possibilities that could have been created.

With several setbacks in my social setting and with a realisation that I was not growing any younger, time had come to open a new page in my life and career.

Those days, anyone making a genuine application seeking employment in another Government Ministry, Department, Agency, Parastatals, Financial Institution, or any Commerce and Industry from the Drug Enforcement Commission (DEC), Special Investigations Team on Economy and Trade (SITET) or Anti-Corruption Commission (ACC) was looked upon as a "plant", some sort of a spy trying to study the operations of the new employers and pass on all the information to the Law Enforcement Agencies.

There was a belief and strong rumours that once you join the ACC, DEC, or some Commission or Department with "Investigative powers" you would never be allowed to resign or leave and you were bonded for life. This fallacy and unsubstantiated belief made it difficult for most qualified officers who have wished to pursue other careers. The ACC or DEC tag could be career limiting for many who have failed to find the escape route from the societal perception bondage which unfortunately is unfounded.

I chose to see that what can be gained was more valuable than what could have been lost. Security is not found by denying or hiding from the changes. Lasting security comes from being able to thrive and prosper, with your integrity intact, no matter what changes may come. Whatever the change of the day or the moment may be, there is a positive response. I challenged myself to find that response, and to make every change a change for the better. Time had come for me to move on. I moved on.

Chapter Four

Investigators Moral and Ethical Quandaries

The questions which beg for honest answers among many others are; how ethical are African Investigators from both the private sector as well as the Public institutions? As individual professionals, let us do some soul searching and introspection as we consider some of the practical challenges Professional Investigators may face or have faced in real life as illustrated in the paragraphs below.

Pre- supposing that you are a Public or Private sector professionally qualified and skilled investigator operating in an African environment, how would you as someone assigned to deal with such scenarios act under any of the following circumstances?

Scenario 1

You have been assigned to investigate a very Senior Politically Exposed Person (PEP) in an African Country, Nation or State. According to the Association of Certified Anti-Money Laundering Specialist (ACAMS) and the Financial Action Task Force (FATF) Recommendation 6 and European Union (EU) Third Anti-Money Laundering Directive, PEPs are "Natural persons who are or have been entrusted with prominent political functions and immediate family members or persons known to be close associates of such persons."(Article 3 (8).

"Individuals who are or have been entrusted with prominent public functions in a foreign country, for example Heads of State or of government, senior politicians, senior government, judicial or military officials, senior executives of state owned corporations, important political party officials."

PEP is a natural person who is or has held an important, influential, prominent and/or senior public or political position(s) with substantial authority over policy, allocation or use of governmental resources e.g. Head of State, Prime Minister, Cabinet Ministers, Supreme and High Court Judges, Senior Military personnel such as Army Commanders, Air force Commanders, National Service Commanders, Inspector Generals of Police, Speakers of National Assembly and Members of Parliament. PEPs include immediate family members and known close associates of such a person.

Interestingly, in most African Countries, the National Constitutions have been crafted in such a way that the most Senior and Highest PEP in the African countries such as Republican Presidents and Prime Ministers have been given the National Constitutional powers and authority have been bestowed upon the said Offices to dutifully appoint many other PEPS in an African setting. Whether ratified, endorsed or rubber stamped by Parliament is another story.

Because of the way African Politics and Democracy have operated since early 1950s to date, these other appointed Senior PEPs have close allegiance to most senior and highest PEP in the Land who in most cases is the President of the Nation or Republic.

The PEP you have been assigned to investigate who is alleged to be a corrupt public official is at Cabinet Minister Level. You can't find the bribe allegedly taken. Is it advisable or permissible to ask your former classmate at Makerere University and girlfriend at the Bank next door to have a look to see if she can find any "round amount" deposits in the PEPs account allegedly deposited as a proceed of crime?

Scenario 2

You are an Anti-Money Laundering (AML), Know Your Customer (KYC) and Customer Due Diligence (CDD), Trade and Economic Sanctions (TES) advisor and Money Laundering Reporting Officer (MLRO) for an International Financial Institution like a Bank listed on several Markets in USA, Europe and Asia. You come across several suspicious transactions and activities for the Republican President's first family, their associates and other very Senior Politically Exposed Persons (PEPs) who are actually sanctioned by the Office of the Foreign Assets Control (OFAC) in the USA and Her Majesty the Treasury (HMT) of the United Kingdom (UK), the United Nations (UN), the European Union (EU) and the African Union (AU).

Among those customers are in fact the Central Bank Governor and Minister of Finance who are also responsible for regulating and issuance of Banking licenses and annual renewals for your Banking license. The Country Anti-Money Laundering (AML) law says you must raise and file a Suspicious Activity Report (SAR) and file it with Regulators such as the Anti-Money Laundering Authority or Investigations Unit, the Central Bank – Bank Supervision or Financial Intelligence Unit (FIU) or Financial Intelligent Centre (FIC).

As a trained and seasoned professional Investigator, you are at the same time aware of the supreme law of the land, the Constitution of the Country which clearly stipulates that the Republican President enjoys immunity from criminal investigations and prosecutions and therefore can't be investigated whilst in the Office. As a fully baked professional investigator, you are also fully aware that the Head of the Financial Intelligence Unit (FIU), the Head of Anti-Money Laundering Authority or the Inspector General of the Police Force or Service where you are supposed to report the matter is in fact a relative to the powers that be and was actually appointed by the people you want to file a report on. What do you do before you damage your Managing Director and Chief Executive Officer (MD/CEO) and the Company's good reputation and image in the eyes of the Regulators who issues and annually renew your company's operating licenses?

Scenario 3

You are a professional investigator from the private sector working in an International Financial Institution. You have been assigned to investigate a hard core but well known and well connected Fraudster and Con artist within the Capital City. Your line manager thinks you are not quick in your turn around time. It is towards the year end. Your annual bonus pay may be affected, reduced or not even be paid out to you as a result of the perceived lethargy and by your inertia to conclude this case.

You are equally and genuinely struggling to trace the fraudster who is alleged to have gone into hiding. Your constraints arise as a result of international law regarding bribes, gifts and entertainment as you can longer pay out lunch allowances, talk time, or provide transport and entertainment to the "Sovereign State" under the Anti-Bribery and Corrupt Act of the UK and USA Foreign Corrupt Practices Act (FCPA). Due to the limited transport resources and high fuel cost, it has been difficult for you to make movements. After all you are no longer allowed to "fund" police operations for them to trace the fraudster on your behalf and you have no authority to effect an arrest.

Is it permissible to use your family contact at Telkom, MTN, Vodacom, Safaricom, and Airtel mobile Company to establish the suspect's address? What do you do since you work in a private sector and you are not allowed to obtain warrants of search from the Courts of Law unless you formally report the case to the Law Enforcement Agency of which the Board of Directors and Senior Management are not of the idea because of negative and adverse media publicity and therefore bad for the business, corporate image and Company if you formally reported the case to Law Enforcement agency?

Scenario 4

You are the Staff Sergeant working in the Homicide Division of the National Police Service or Police Force. You are interviewing a murder suspect number three. Accompanied by his Lawyer/Attorney, the suspect decides and opts to exercise his National Constitutional right to remain silent. The suspect does not want to confess the criminal doing. From experience and from earlier interrogations of other accomplices and suspects, you very well know or strongly suspect that he is the ring leader who committed the alleged offence of suspected ritual murders where body parts such as the heart, breasts and private parts have been missing from those brutally killed.

Fully knowing that human rights abuse of beating the suspect to confess may backfire against you, would it be advisable to call the bluff by telling him that Suspects number one and two had already confessed and provided incriminating evidence about him?

As you consider this scenario, just bear in mind the limited resources for the African Investigator. Most of rural and Community Police Posts have no Closed Circuit

Televisions (CCTV) cameras in most of the places. Even where CCTVs are available, there could have been affected by power deficit and load shedding. There is also not enough transport, surveillance equipment and record keeping systems including access records.

Scenario 5

You are a Certified Fraud Examiner (CFE) who has read and fully understood the Professional Code of Ethics and Conduct very well. You are conducting a Fraud Risk Assessment (FRA) in a Publically Listed Company (PLC). You stumble upon Management information and data which clearly gives you some great insight to some sensitive information.

It is now clear in your mind that the same company you are professionally examining and assessing would be going insolvent or bankrupt anytime sooner rather than later. You equally know that your own father-in-law holds one million shares in this now shaky company.

Would it be right for you to advise your wife to tell her father to sell his shares due to market conditions before he makes a loss? Remember that your lovely and dear wife and children would also loose through inheritance since everything has been bequeathed to your wife as the only daughter to your rich father-in-law.

Scenario 6

You are the Head of Financial Crime Risk and Compliance Manager in a blue chip International Banking and Financial Institution. Your Managing Director and Chief Executive Officer (MD/CEO) had given you an assignment to investigate the net worth assets of one of the Executive management Committee (EXCO) members whom it has been alleged had been taking bribes and kickbacks from outsourced contractors and suppliers.

A few days later the suspect approaches you and asks you directly in your face whether you are investigating her. Is it alright to tell her that you are not doing an investigation, but just doing a procurement review? Or do you get the audacity to go back and establish whether the MD/CEO had breached levels of confidentiality and shared with the suspect the investigations instituted but instigated by the same MD/CEO against the other Executive Committee member?

Scenario 7

Your uncoordinated, disorganised and probably laziest colleague or friend and former school mate is also facing several disciplinary cases within the same institution asks you if you would be her referee. She is applying for a new well paying big job as Director of Human Resources within a competitor Institution. The Executive Talent recruitment company calls you directly for your recommendation and assessment. What do you tell them?

Scenario 8

For your professional execution of investigative assignments in Africa, you needed to and you ordered brand new surveillance and recording gadgets from an internet-vendor based in the mainland Greater China. The package which arrives in-Country contains two sets of gadgets, but you only ordered and paid for one. You are based in Southern Africa. What do you do?

Scenario 9

Because of limited Office space in the sitting arrangement nowadays, the colleague sitting at the desk next to you does not log-off from his e-mail before he leaves for lunch.

You have been suspecting that he is having an affair with a married senior Human Resource Manager within the Company who has caused professional Hell on Earth in your life before by denying you promotion, bonus and departmental transfers for several years now. What do you do?

Scenario 10

You are the Head of a Department. During the Company arranged Town Hall or Road Show, the Managing Director and Chief Executive Officer or Inspector General of Police calls you in front of everybody and praises you openly for a very good investigations and for compiling an excellent report.

In the heart of your hearts, you know you did not compile this particular report being referred to. The report was actually written by one of your brilliant subordinates. What do you say to your boss and who takes the credit for the promotion and Bonus?

Chapter Five

Doing Right Even When No One Is Looking

From the ten scenarios highlighted Chapter Four, (4) we can see that as Investigators, Inspectors and Examiners, we can go on and on with such practical and real life ethical and moral temptations and dilemmas in our Professional careers. Be that as it may, the moral direct question to all of us is, is it ethically correct to bend the rules in the professional investigators game against criminal suspects and our investigations?

Ethics by the way comes from the Greek word "ETHOS" which means "character". Socrates posited that people will naturally do what is good if they know what is right. He further correlated knowledge with virtue and similarly equated virtue with happiness.

But, from the African perspective, is it true that "the truly wise man will know what is right, do what is good, be content and therefore be happy?" That would be good for the ears of some of our fine Religions of the World including Christianity, Islam, Hindu, Taoism, Buddhism, atheists and free thinkers but that is another dimension for another day.

Last time we checked on Wikipanion, ethics were being referred to as moral philosophy, a branch of philosophy that involves systematising, defending and recommending concepts of right and wrong conduct.

According to Richard Paul and Linda Elder of the Foundation for Critical Thinking, they define ethics as a "set of concepts and principles that guide us in determining what behaviour helps or harms sentiment creatures".

The Cambridge Dictionary of Philosophy states that the word ethics is "commonly used interchangeably with "morality" and sometimes it is used more narrowly to mean the moral principles of a particular tradition, group or individual".

Whether you deal with Anti-Money Laundering (AML), Counter-Terrorism Financing(CTF), Anti-Bribery and Corruption (ABC), Financial Crime Risk (FCR), Drug Enforcement Commission/Agency (DEC/A), Financial Intelligence Centre/Unit (FIC/U), Fraud Risk Management and Investigations, public or Private Sector, Private Eye type of investigations and surveillances, Clandestine Operations and mercenary work, for the professional and qualified African investigators, Ethics can be said to be a set of personal rules, above and beyond the laws or policies that govern our beloved industry.

Ethics also ensure that we do what is right in all circumstances, with our nucleus and extended family, friends and colleagues, suspects, witnesses, office mates and staff, company, shareholders, suppliers, customers, and competitors alike.

For all those in the calling, good ethics, I believe and strongly so should enable all of our decisions to stand up to scrutiny over the long term, by a person of the highest integrity, common sense, the Constitution and humanity.

The African Continent is a strange part of the World. Things happen differently. Collection of a person's beliefs and morals makes up a set of principles known as ethics. Ethics could be used as the sound judgments about what is right and wrong or, more specifically, a person's moral obligations to society. That being the case would obviously determine a person's actions in our chosen field.

In the African Political setting however, determining

ethical rights and wrongs is complicated by the fact that moral standards and generally accepted social behaviour change with time. That may depend on the Political Party ruling at the time and setting the tone from the top for all the citizens and cares alike.

If for example, the high ranking and those in the echelons and corridors of power are perceived to be on a wanton and primitive crusade of accumulating corruptly acquired wealth, then the moral campus and ethics shifts to such a low standard to the extent that everyone doing wrong things is deemed to be conforming to the societal and socially acceptable norms. In such a scenario anyone trying to raise the bar and remind others of the biblical beatitudes is perceived to be carrying a holier than thou attitude and much scorn is showered upon such wretched soul.

Cognisant of the fact that, modernization, globalisation, global influence may vary the ethics and morals from one section of society to another, Country to Country, Province to Province, District to District, Town to Town, Constituency to Constituency, Tribe to Tribe, Clan to Clan and maybe from profession to profession, we as Professionals need to fully identify and be aware of our own professional ethics and morals.

In addition, different groups in the same society or a Country may have conflicting ideas of right and wrong. For instance, a perceived dangerous criminal and robber ready to be burnt alive with a tyre ring on his neck by an instant mob justice suspected to be hard core, serial and ritual killer/criminal by investigators and prosecutors may be perceived by defence Lawyers and local law firms as a good client whose human rights is being infringed upon by his uncalled for, inhuman and unlawful incarceration by the state machinery.

A common fallacy which may arise in discussing ethics is "If it's legal, it's ethical." A common defence to charges of unethical behaviour is to invoke the law. This legalistic approach to ethics mistakenly implies that actions that are not explicitly prohibited by the law are ethical. This to our Investigative profession should be deemed as a very wrong dimension of looking at ethics.

The main error in this approach is that legal standards do not establish ethical principles. Although abiding by the law is a part of ethical behaviour, laws themselves do not describe how unethical person should behave.

In an African setting, one can be dishonest, gay, unprincipled, untrustworthy, unfair, lesbian and uncaring without breaking the law depending on which Country you are referring to.

Moral philosophy deals with choices between what is good against what is evil and right against what is wrong.

There maybe two basic approaches to this debate:

(a) "Moral absolutism" requires morals and values to be universally accepted, and not even change over time

(b) "Moral relativism" this behaviour is acceptable as long as your specific industry or society condones it, regardless of what other societies think.

Kindly allow me to insist that with African Professional Investigators and I'm using this term very broadly and loosely to encompass many specialised fields and people dealing in many and various predicate and serious offences, "Integrity means doing the right thing, even if nobody is watching". Imagine that with the relatively low pay and high bribes offers from the corrupt and financially loaded money launderers.

Ethical dilemmas occur when:

a) A situation of conflict of interest arises. Remember to refer to your dear wife and father in law scenario in a previous chapter.

b) Alternatives and other options are available with different outcomes.

c) The correct decision is not clear in terms of moral principles. (Report the First Family and you and your MD/CEO risk being fired by the Board)

d) The potential prejudice to one/some.

e) The potential benefit to the decision-maker (Bonus and Promotion at risk if you do not call a friend from the mobile Company for an address of your main suspect).

f) Whether the truth will eventually become known (You or subordinate wrote a report but being rewarded).

As African Professional investigators we should at all times:

a) Consider the facts and the evidence as being more important than suspicions or perceptions and other prejudices we may hold.

b) Conduct all investigations with integrity and professionalism.

c) Be honest in all professional interactions even when your boss, your junior or no one is watching.

d) Strive to report those engaging in Money Laundering, Bribery, Corruption, Plunder of National and Natural resources, embezzlement, skimming, phishing, theft, misappropriation, fraud or deception to appropriate authorities.

One may ask how can an ethical behaviour by the Anti-Corruption Commission/Bureau Investigator hurt or destroy a bribery case. Others have argued that "It can't". Officers may use all available means, including excessive force and unethical behaviour, to resolve an investigation.

While in an interview room for example, if you are uncooperative like what one Minister of Justice did in one Southern African Country where he went with Party cadres and supporters demanding that the Anti-Corruption Commissioner interviews him in public domain, in full view of the National Television cameras and his Party cadres/supporters, professional investigators are put in a very awkward moral and ethical dilemmas. That is for another day.

In Africa, if the suspect is a lesser mortal, Investigators may utilize things such as unconventional "Guantanamo bay" type of interrogation depending on the severity of the case such as those leading to economic sabotage and treasonable offences. Tactics such as hanging from the rope or swing upside down (kampelwa in one of the Southern African Country) or some "shock therapy" and talking about doing things with your wife, mother, mother in-law and/or sister to ensure that you talk or reveal the details of the actual criminal case.

Be mindful if you are the main suspect that if you ask for an attorney/lawyer, investigators are only obligated to comply with that request if an officer is present in the room with his official uniform hat on and an Official badge number on.

Some African Investigators with limited resources and gadgets at their disposal have been known to have used fear, stress, deception and their networks illegally to obtain confessions and proceed to prosecute matter in courts of law with illegally obtained evidence and confessions under duress.

Coming to institutional and organizational arrangements, these values and ethics of an individual are reflected in their actions as employees.

There are four factors that generally affect the ethical decisions of employees:

a) The law and other government regulations.

b) Industry and organizational ethical codes.

c) Social pressures.

d) Tension between personal standards and organizational needs

One of the easiest ways to establish a strong moral tone for an organization is to hire morally sound employees. The concept of Know Your Employees (KYE) is cardinal here. Too often, the hiring process is conducted in a slipshod manner.

Chapter Six

Drain The Swamps, Never Fight The Alligators

Organizations should conduct thorough background checks on all new employees, especially managers and directors. In addition, it is important to conduct thorough interviews with applicants to ensure that they have adequate skills to perform the duties that will be required of them. Know Your Employee (KYE). Identify the enemy within.

Fraud prevention requires a system of rules, which, in their aggregate, minimize the likelihood of fraud occurring while maximizing the possibility of detecting any fraudulent activity that may transpire.

Professional investigators very well know that the potential of being caught most often persuades likely perpetrators not to commit the fraud. Because of this principle, the existence of a thorough control system is essential to fraud prevention. It is cheaper to drain the swamps than fight the alligators and crocodiles. Take heed.

No control environment will be effective unless there is consistent discipline for ethical violations. Consistent discipline requires a well-defined set of sanctions for violations, and strict adherence to the prescribed disciplinary measures. If one employee is punished for an act within the Finance Department and another employee is not punished for a similar act just because he or she comes from the Operations and Administration Department, then be rest assured that the moral force of the company's ethics policy will be diminished.

We must all remember that Laws were established from the outset of civilization as people will always "push the boundaries." All Staff in an organization without exception therefore need to know what those boundaries are. Leaving members of staff to guess and speculate is courting disaster.

Those who have been long in this field when carrying out investigations or disciplinary process have heard sometimes from those being interviewed that "I didn't know that was wrong – where does it say I cannot do that?"

It is imperative for every institution to set out in black and white exactly what is acceptable and what is not. Staff will be put on notice that certain behaviour is unacceptable. The key is to prevent the staff that has been recruited from straying from the "straight and narrow" and go off the rails.

The aim of a Code of Ethics policy is to demonstrate to both employees and the outside world that any Organisation or Institutions is taking the threat of Anti-Money laundering, (AML), Counter Terrorism Financing (CTF), Financial Crime Risk (FCR), dishonesty, fraud, and theft seriously.

By issuing a detailed Staff policy and procedures, we need as professionals to aid our Employers to clearly set out what is considered to be dishonest. Such Policies would also warn any potential wrongdoers that the consequences of being caught will be serious. The effect therefore will be to deter any potential wrongdoers thus resulting in reduced losses from any wrongdoing and reduced costs in respect of investigating any wrongdoing.

As a polite reminder to all those involved in investigations on the African Continent, it is professionally acceptable to respect the wishes of witnesses, colleagues, and professionals. We should safeguard confidentiality and privacy of people, documents and companies.

The African Investigator is encouraged to continue to

study, apply and advance scientific knowledge, to observe the precepts of accuracy and prudence and to make relevant information available to colleagues and the public when permitted by law.

We just as investigators must strive to always respect the law and legal authority. We must not reveal any confidential information obtained during a professional assignment without proper authorisation.

Inevitably, when we are called upon by law, like during the trial by the courts of law, we must reveal all material matters discovered during the course of an investigation, which, if omitted, could cause a distortion of the facts and lead to a miscarriage of justice by Magistrates and Judges setting the guilty free on the basis of technicalities.

We should also continually strive to increase the ethical content of services performed under our jurisdictions and direction.

Some of our relatively new comers to the calling may wish to know how to tell and know whether their actions are right? The following questions can be applied as a guideline of whether it is acceptable or not:

a) Does the conduct comply with the law of the land or company policy and procedures?

b) Does the conduct comply with the Professional and universally Code of Ethics?

c) What would the public think if this action is reported in the electronic and print media?

d) What would your superiors say about this action? What about family and colleagues?

e) Does the result of this action feel right and fair?

Some guidance and constant reminders to all of us may

not be a bad idea. Treat the suspect the way you would have liked to be treated (not under state of emergency). Consider the perception of third parties (Courts of Law, Defence Counsel, Superiors, Press and Labour Laws, Workers Union and Human Resource Policies). Always stay within the law.

The ethical key for us is to keep emotions and feelings of anger and betrayal towards all suspects in balance. None in the field of investigations can afford to let personal fears and hatred of crime control the situations with such suspects.

If allowed to become unprofessional or unethical, it opens a whole new set of problems in the cases worked on. That invariably allow criminals to not be convicted of the crimes they commit on the basis of legal technicalities. That can lead to even more crimes, being committed by the same offenders. Care must be taken to ensure the situation does not arise to free such suspects from the hands of justice.

The thankless but noble calling and Professional African Investigators in all fields are being encouraged to continue to "Always be honest, tell the truth about everything, never exaggerate or misrepresent what you know or what you are doing during your investigations"

Chapter Seven

Birth - Institute of Directors (IoD) in Zambia

G ood Corporate Governance and structures in various companies, institutions and organisations supplement efforts to combat financial criminal activities. This is the vivid re-collection of the momentous occasion in Zambia. This is how the journey of corporate governance started in Zambia.

In the cold winter month of June 1998, in Lusaka, Zambia, Commonwealth Programme on Corporate Governance and the Commonwealth Association for Corporate Governance in collaboration with the Commonwealth Fund for Technical Co-operation and the Institute of Chartered Secretaries and Administrators (Zambia Association) organised a three (3) day workshop at Intercontinental hotel in Lusaka.

The workshop attracted key stakeholders from across a spectrum of various sectors of the Zambian Society with different professional backgrounds. Government of the Republic of Zambia Officials, Businessmen and women, Parastatal Companies, Commissions, Agencies and Civil Societies were present.

Mr. Michael Gillibrand was a Special Adviser Management and Training Services Division at Commonwealth Secretariat. Mr. Mohan Thomas was

Chairman of the Institute of Chartered Secretaries and Administrators whereas Mr. Geoffrey Bowes was the Executive Director for Commonwealth Association for Corporate Governance.

The three day interactive and power point slide presentation (remember that Microsoft PowerPoint slide presentations using projectors with fancy flying animations sounding like type writers or emergency car breaks had just been introduced in Zambia) was both educative and enlightening.

Among the notable presenters who inspired the audience and workshop participants was a fine gentleman by the name of Boyman Mankama from the neighbouring Country Zimbabwe. The man was so passionate about Corporate Governance not only in Companies but Government Institutions. He was a good orator too.

This was the time Comrade Robert Gabriel Mugabe His Excellency the President of the Republic of Zimbabwe and his Cabinet Ministers and Parliamentarians had just passed a law on Land reforms in that Country. The "Zimbabwean White Farmers" had started trooping away from that Country to neighbouring Countries including Zambia. The resounding round of applause was phenomenal. The author of this book has kept notes from various presenters of the workshop for posterity and future generations to be inspired as well.

One most important and cardinal action point and way forward of this ground breaking workshop was a firm resolution to assemble a "TASK FORCE" on the formation of the INSTITUTE of DIRECTORS (IoD) in Zambia.

This collection of fine brains and minds was established in June 1998 by the Institute of Chartered Secretaries in Zambia with the specific responsibilities of drawing up a Code of Ethics/Code of Conduct (COE/COC), the constitution, rules for the IoD of Zambia and incorporating the Organisation.

The work of the Task Force was studied and debated

extensively by the panel of professional Lawyers, Accountants, Bankers and those from the Law Enforcement who distilled the thoughts, drafts, and recommendations into the Code of Conduct and Corporate practices in Zambia.

The Chairman recorded his thanks and appreciation for the work done by the Task Force Team members and the Committee. The task Force among others had an enviable task of studying the Codes of Best Practice, the various constitutions which were received from the Institutes of Directors in New Zealand, Zimbabwean and South Africa.

Hundreds of Hours went into the wading of physical papers, files, reports, documents, the Studies of the Literature, the Codes of Conduct, the Codes of Ethics, Corporate Governance and what it entails. Various research papers and journal publications, constitutions from the Republics of South Africa, Zimbabwe, The United kingdom, Australia and New Zealand were reviewed with the aspiration recommendations from which the Code of Ethics, Code of Conduct and the ultimately the Constitution to form IOD in Zambia evolved.

Just to confirm that there were no effective Internet browsing and bandwidth was not broad enough to Google search on such subjects. Hence, there was heavy reliance on some paperwork, published articles, magazines, journals, land telephone lines and physical letters moving correspondence through the Post Offices and messengers to communicate with others in-country and our colleagues who were outside the Countries:

- Some Salient Lessons learnt was that corporate governance in South Africa was institutionalised by the publication of the King Report on Corporate Governance ("King Report 1994") in November 1994. Mervyne E. King (S.C.) was the Chairman of the Committee.

- The King Committee on Corporate Governance was formed in 1992, under the auspices of the Institute of Directors, to consider corporate governance, of increasing interest around the world.

- You will recall or read the History of South Africa that this coincided with profound social and political transformation at the time with the dawning of democracy and the re-admission of South Africa into the community of nations and the world economy.

- The purpose of the King Report 1994 was, and remains, to promote the highest standards of corporate governance in South Africa. Unlike its counterparts in other countries at the time, the King Report 1994 went beyond the financial and regulatory aspects of corporate governance in advocating an integrated approach to good governance in the interests of a wide range of stakeholders having regard to the fundamental principles of good financial, social, ethical and environmental practice.

- In adopting a participative corporate governance system of enterprise with integrity, the King Committee in 1994 successfully formalised the need for companies to recognise that they no longer act independently from the societies and the environment in which they operate.

- A distinction was clearly made between accountability and responsibility: One is liable to render an account when one is accountable and one is liable to be called to account when one is responsible.

- We learnt that the modern approach is for a board to identify the company's stakeholders, including its shareowners, and to agree on policies as to how the relationship with those stakeholders should be advanced and managed in the interests of the company.

- Corporate discipline is a commitment by a company's senior management to adhere to behaviour that is universally recognised and accepted to be correct and proper. This encompasses a company's awareness of, and commitment to, the underlying principles of good governance, particularly at senior management level.

- Transparency on the other hand is the ease with which an outsider is able to make meaningful analysis of a company's actions, its economic fundamentals and the non-financial aspects pertinent to that business.

- This is a measure of how good management is at making necessary information available in a candid, accurate and timely manner – not only the audit data but also general reports and press releases. It reflects whether or not investors obtain a true picture of what is happening inside the company. Remember that the Zambia Privatisation Program was at its peak during that period.

- Independence is the extent to which mechanisms have been put in place to minimise or avoid potential conflicts of interest that may exist, such as dominance by a strong chief executive or large shareowner.

- These mechanisms range from the composition of the board, to appointments to committees of the board, and external parties such as the auditors.

- Individuals or groups in a company, who make decisions and take actions on specific issues, need to be accountable for their decisions and actions.

- Mechanisms must exist and be effective to allow for accountability. These provide investors with the means to query and assess the actions of the board and its committees. With regard to management, responsibility pertains to behaviour that allows for corrective action and for penalising mismanagement.

- Responsible management would, when necessary, put in place what it would take to set the company on the right path. While the board is accountable to the company, it must act responsively to and with responsibility towards all stakeholders of the company.

Corporate Governance has also been recognised as an effective mechanism for encouraging efficiency, fighting financial crime, corporate fraud, abuse of official positions, combating bribery and corruption.

By the way Anti-Corruption Commission (ACC) was invited to this workshop and Mrs. Agnes Kayobo Ngandu – The Director of Corruption Prevention and Community Education Division and the Senior Manager and Head of The Corruption Prevention Department then Kunda Emmanuel Kalaba were among those present. Their contribution during the workshop was very useful.

Although, it has been recognised that Countries and communities differ in their culture, regulation, law and generally the way business is done, the World Bank has pointed out, there can be no single generally applicable corporate governance model, yet there are international standards that no country can escape in the era of the global investor.

International guidelines have been developed by the Organisation for Economic Co-operation and Development (OECD), the International Corporate Governance Network, and the Commonwealth Association for Corporate Governance. The four primary pillars of fairness, accountability, responsibility and transparency are fundamental to all these international guidelines of corporate governance.

The board is the focal point of the corporate governance system. It is ultimately accountable and responsible for the performance and affairs of the company. Delegating authority to board committees or management does not in any way mitigate or dissipate the discharge by the board and its directors of their duties and responsibilities.

The board must give strategic direction to the company, appoint the chief executive officer and ensure that succession is planned. The board must retain full and effective control over the company, and monitor management in implementing board plans and strategies. The board should ensure that the company complies with all relevant laws, regulations and codes of business practice, and that it communicates with its shareowners and relevant stakeholders (internal and external) openly and promptly and with substance prevailing over form.

The board should have unrestricted access to all company information, records, documents and property. The information needs of the board should be well defined and regularly monitored. The board should consider developing a corporate code of conduct that addresses conflicts of interest, particularly relating to directors and management, which should be regularly reviewed and updated as necessary.

The board must identify key risk areas and key performance indicators of the business enterprise. These should be regularly monitored, with particular attention given to technology and systems.

The board should encourage shareowners to attend annual general meetings and other company meetings, at which the directors should be present. More particularly, the chairpersons of each of the board's committees, especially the audit and remuneration committees should be present at the annual general meeting.

A brief Curriculum Vitae (CV) or Resume of each director standing for election or re-election at the annual general meeting should accompany the notice contained in the annual report.

Every board should have a charter setting out its responsibilities, which should be disclosed in its annual report. At a minimum, the charter should confirm the board's responsibility for the adoption of strategic plans, monitoring of operational performance and management, determination of policy and processes to ensure the integrity of the company's risk management and internal controls, communications policy, and director selection, orientation and evaluation.

Non-executive directors should be individuals of caliber and credibility, and have the necessary skill and experience to bring judgment to bear independent of management, on issues of strategy, performance, resources, transformation, diversity and employment equity, standards of conduct and evaluation of performance.

The board should meet regularly, at least once a quarter if not more frequently as circumstances require, and should disclose in the annual report the number of board and committee meetings held in the year and the details of attendance of each director (as applicable).

The board is responsible for the total process of risk management, as well as for forming its own opinion on the effectiveness of the process. Management is accountable to the board for designing, implementing and monitoring the process of risk management and integrating it into the day-to-day activities of the company.

Every company should engage its stakeholders in determining the company's standards of ethical behaviour. It should demonstrate its commitment to organisational integrity by codifying its standards in a code of ethics.

"Corporate governance is concerned with holding the balance between economic and social goals and between individual and communal goals...the aim is to align as nearly as possible the interests of individuals, corporations and society." Sir Adrian Cadbury - , Corporate Governance Overview, 1999 -World Bank Report.

It is now generally accepted by multinationals operating in various jurisdictions that "demonstrating concern creates an atmosphere of trust and a better understanding of corporate aims, so that when the next crisis comes (and these are inevitable for big companies) there will be a greater goodwill to help the company survive".

The decisions made, and internal processes established, should be objective and not allow for undue influences. This reminds us of the legendary Messrs. Francis Kaunda and Edward Shamutete the once mighty Director Generals under ZIMCO Group of Companies. The duo was both great Chairmen and Chief Executive Officers of the once great company – Zambia Consolidated Copper Mines (ZCCM).

I had personally met them in their Official capacities in this huge Office at Mukuba House off Dedan Kimathi road near the Government Complex Building which was initially constructed as the UNIP Headquarters under the all very powerful Dr. Kenneth David Kaunda's era.

As a younger man then with full of energy and eager to learn from the Elders and Chief Executives sitting for the first time in one of the posh Board Room recently refurbished, I was personally inspired to work on this Task Force Committee by the fact that so many prominent Zambian with very prominent positions obviously with very busy work and social schedules to attend to, gave of their precious and valuable time on honorary basis.

Meetings were held at Zambia Privatisation House (ZPA) now Zambia Development Agency (ZDA) near the New Government Complex House offices after official working hours. Meetings would run from 18.30hrs running all the way up to and beyond 22.00hrs depending on the agenda items on a bi-weekly basis.

None of the Task Force members even attempted to claim or recover their personal disbursements in drafting the Zambian COE, COC and the Constitution of the IOD. Those days "sitting allowances" in workshops and meetings was the in thing during the Frederick Titus Jacob Chiluba's rule as the President of the Republic of Zambia. We all proudly sacrificed and did it for the love of mother Zambia.

As of September 14th 1998, the Interim Task Force members who used to meet at Zambia Privatization Agency Board room after 18.00hrs and worked tirelessly to ensure IOD was created were; Mr. Patrick D. Chisanga – Chairman, Mr. Kenneth Chibesakunda, Ms. Joyce Muwo, Mrs. Mary T. Ncube, Mr. Mohan Thomas, Mr. Kunda E. Kalaba, Mrs. Elizabeth Jere, Mr. Michael Daka, Mr. Stephen Ndhlovu, Mr. Charles Mate, Mr. Satish Gulati, Dr.

Herrick Mphuku, Mr. Luke Mbewe, Mr. Robert Mwambwa, Mr. Mumba Kapumpa, Mr. Isaac Ponde, Mr. Fabian C. Lukashi (Secretary).

As Zambians are no doubt fully aware, "we have successfully put together a Constitution for the IOD of Zambia and we have also incorporated it as a Company limited by guarantee under the Companies Act.

In short, we have delivered our mandate in full, In thanking you for the excellent work done, I think that it is also appropriate that I should announce the formal dissolution of the Task Force, In consequence, I am by copy of this letter advising the Chairman of the ICSA (Stephen Ndhlovu, FCIS) to proceed with the appointment of an interim Board of Directors of the Institute so that it can commence functioning" stated Mr. Patrick D. Chisanga (FCIS) who was Chairman Task Force on the formation of the Institute of Directors in Zambia on 10th February 2000.

In normal societies similar to ours, all the above should be considered and probably "Honoured" with at least life "HONOURALY" membership of the IOD Zambia for being pioneers and Founding Fathers and Mothers of IOD Zambia which was established in the new millennium – January 2000 to be specific.

It is not too late to ask or consider. This is the best way we can honour and say excellent and or job well done for your selfless sacrifice and unflinching support for the two (2) year long period of hard work which ensured that the desired result of formation or creation of the IOD is established and flourishes in its operations in Zambia. I just thought of putting the record straight for the new generation and generations to come.

Corporate governance is at the heart of most of the

issues that have arisen thus far in Zambia and beyond. The Task Force members were very passionate about this subject.

In the information age everyone, willingly or not, is a member of the global market place. Concepts like Globalisation were just reaching Zambia and proponents like Messrs. Elias Chipimo Junior and the late Mebelo Mutukwa argued that as members of this global club, everyone lives in a borderless world, not one as envisaged by the World Trade Organisation with no geographic trading borders but one where information crosses borders with the "click of a mouse". Relying on this information, capital flows across geographic borders as if they were nonexistent. Zambia just has to play her part.

In more than twenty Countries the author has travelled to and visited globally, he has come to conclude that any information being channeled out from any Country must be trustworthy before an investor can convince other partners and before arriving at any life changing decision to move money and invest the same somewhere else on this earth.

The measurement for this trust and confidence is the quality of the governance of the company imparting the information. The implications for companies are profound. Simply by developing good governance practices, Chief Executive Officers, Chief Financial Officer, Risk Director, Legal and Compliance Managers, Corporate and Company Secretaries and other Senior Managers can potentially add significant shareowner value.

It should be apparent to the Policy makers and regulators in recognising that the creation of a good governance climate can make countries, especially in the developing and emerging markets, a magnet for global capital. Companies not only need to be well-governed, but also need to be perceived in the market as being well governed. We surely need more Zambian Companies to be listed at International markets. They can start at Lusaka Stock Exchange (LUSE) and go further on other International Markets.

If there is a lack of good corporate governance in a market, capital will leave that market with the click of a mouse. The recent Foreign Exchange rates speak volumes.

As Arthur Levitt, the former Chairperson of the USA Securities and Exchange Commission has said, "If a country does not have a reputation for strong corporate governance practices, capital will flow elsewhere. If investors are not confident with the level of disclosure, capital will flow elsewhere. If a country opts for lax accounting and reporting standards, capital will flow elsewhere. All enterprises in that country – regardless of how steadfast a particular company's practices may be – suffer the consequences. Markets must now honour what they perhaps, too often, have failed to recognise. Markets exist by the grace of investors. And it is today's more empowered investors that will determine which companies and which markets will stand the test of time and endure the weight of greater competition. It serves us well to remember that no market has a divine right to investors' capital".

The collective desire for each and every company registered and incorporated in Zambia by the Patents and Company Registration Agency (PACRA) is that each company (including Small and Medium Enterprises (SMEs) should demonstrate its commitment to its code of ethics by communicating with, and training, all employees regarding enterprise values, standards and compliance procedures; creating systems and procedures to introduce, monitor and enforce its ethical code; assigning high level individuals to oversee compliance to the ethical code; assessing the integrity of new appointees in the selection and promotion procedures; exercising due care in delegating discretionary authority; providing, monitoring and auditing safe systems for reporting of unethical or risky behaviour; enforcing appropriate discipline with consistency; and responding to offences and preventing re-occurrence.

It is our ardent hope and prayer that one day, some International Organisations, major investors and institutions would come to Zambia and say Zambia has the best governance of listed companies in emerging economies. That would be fundamental and adequate reward for our work if in the future, Zambian Directors of our Lusaka Stoke Exchange (LUSE) listed Companies and those unlisted companies continue to be recognised as practitioners of good corporate governance.

It will be better than adequate if all affected companies including the Small and Medium Enterprises (SMEs) implemented the Code of Corporate Practices and Conduct their Business in accordance with vision of the Task Force Committee which created the Institute of Directors (IoD) Zambian Chapter . It sounds farfetched but it is doable. Yes, we can!

Chapter Eight

The New Millennium Y2K "Star of Africa"

Between 1990 and 1999, I met most of the Cabinet Ministers, Deputy and Provincial Ministers and the Permanent Secretaries and their Directors under Dr. Kenneth Kaunda and Dr. Frederick Titus Jacob Chiluba in my Official capacity to resolve matters of national interest. I had the rare privilege of picking up a phone and directly call any Managing Director or Chief Executive Officer of both the Private and Public Institution and secure an appointment to meet either in their Office, my Office and any other convenient hotel for a "friendly discussion".

Young and energetic young man, I enjoyed my work but time had come to move on and secure the future of my wife and family. After all, I had married with two lovely daughters by 1999. Our first born daughter was born in October 1994 and the Second daughter was born in September 1999. I tendered my letter of resignation from Anti-Corruption Commission in December 1999.

My mentor and mother–figure Mrs. Agnes Kayobo Ngandu insisted to have an exit interview with me just to establish what future career plans I had if any. She, just like my wife and other family members were worried that I was leaving a very "stable and secure job in Government" and opting to go into "untested, unstable and unsecure job environment in a private sector". Those sentiments have been generally strong which have made some of our Senior citizens and colleagues to serve one Institution for the rest of their careers ranging from one year to forty years.

Admittedly, the risk I took of changing jobs after serving Government for 9 years was huge considering the fact that the new offer of the job I was taking was only one year contract subject to renewal if the Company was satisfied with my performance.

The most worrying concern for everyone was "what if the new employers do not renew the contract, what next?" My response to all those who posed this question was "what if the new employers renewed the contract and put me on permanent and pensionable employment contract?"

I was looking at the glass half full whereas my colleagues and family members may have been looking at half empty glass. "Why fail to perform when you have family responsibilities?" Why not learn quickly, adapt and focus on new assignments, tasks, job role, job description, and job execution?

There is another life outside Government circles. There are only a few ways out. If you overstay in one working place or environment, you become part of the furniture. Eventually, what was once a comfortable retreat becomes a prison? If you continue to deny and avoid the opportunities to move forward, you will eventually find the situation so intolerable that you'll do whatever is necessary to get yourself out of it. Unfortunately, by the time that happens you will have lost many of your best options.

I strongly believe in the concept that as a human being, you must be your greatest asset. Put your time, effort and money into training, grooming, and encouraging your greatest asset – you yourself. Allow your abilities to blossom somewhere else.

Progress is made by those who have the courage to be wrong and the persistence to find how to get it right. Great achievements are crafted into existence by those who, when they begin, are not sure exactly how they'll do it. Don't wait until you know how to do everything before you have the confidence to do anything. Find confidence in the authenticity of your desire and the goodness of your purpose.

You don't have to already be an expert to gain expertise. You just have to get busy. If you should stumble a lot at first, get back up each time and apply what you've just learned. Even when you stumble going forward, you're still moving ahead. Don't wait for confidence to somehow come to you. Get out there and create it for yourself. I consoled myself that I was worthy and able to reach the goals that truly meant something for me. I got myself going, and enjoyed the experience of allowing my capabilities and abilities to blossom.

"In the long run, we shape our lives, and we shape ourselves. The process never ends until we die. And the choices we make are ultimately our responsibility" Eleanor Roosevelt. I had to move. It did not matter at that point whether it was moving sideways or forward, but certainly, the moving was not going backwards.

I began working for Barclays Bank Zambia Plc on the 2nd day of January 2000. The Y2K hype had just settled. I worked for Barclays Bank Zambia Plc, first as Assistant Manager and later as Barclays Africa Security Investigative Services - Manager Fraud Prevention, Investigations and Security at Barclays Bank in Zambia and supporting Southern African Countries.

I was responsible for all Financial Crimes Deterrence, Detection, Prevention, Investigations and prosecutions. The liaison and point of contact with all the Regulators and Law Enforcement Agencies including my Former Employers Anti-Corruption Commission.

I would occasionally take my Former Line Managers and Colleagues for dinners, lunch and drink-up at the famous, popular and prestigious Barclays Bank Manager's Club on Friday evening for relaxing and winding up. I was the Custodian of Bank Security Policies and procedures, Healthy and safety, Bank asset Protection, tracing and making Recoveries, Human Resource (Staff and Customer security), sourcing, contractual obligations of procurement, installations and maintenance of Security and electronic equipment and systems i.e. Access Control and CCTVs.

My line Manager Mr. Charles Lengalenga (the late) and Mr. Richard Beardsall were impressed with my performance which led to His Honour Mr. William Mweemba who was the Head of Legal and Company Secretary to change the contractual terms from 1 year to permanent and pensionable. The Director of Human Resources Mr. Bursch Nketani was in concurrence and fears and concerns by family members and former bosses at Anti-Corruption Commission were put at ease by Christmas time of 2000.

The following year in 2001, I was declared the first (1st) ever prize Gold Eagle Award winner of the Brain Waves and Eagle Award for outstanding performance. I was also awarded the first *"Star of Zambia"* at the Barclays Bank of Zambia Brain Waves and Eagle Awards dinner dance at Inter-Continental Hotel.

Apart from winning a weekend for two (wife and I) at newly opened Protea Hotel in Chisamba, Barclays Bank sponsored me to go to London in the United Kingdom and represented Zambia at the exclusive *"best of the best - Stars of Africa"* dinner hosted by Mr. Chris Lendrum, Chief Executive Corporate Banking PLC, Mr. Dominic Bruynseels, Managing Director of Barclays Africa and Middle East and other top Barclays Executives. Barclays Bank was just in the process of moving the Head Office from the Lombard Street to Canary Wharf.

Here I was, on Business Class of the British Airways going to visit Great Britain. The Official schedule afforded me an opportunity to visit and tour among many other interesting places in London such as the Buckingham Palace, the London Castle, the London Eye, 10 Downing Street, Big Ben, some shopping vouchers dished out to use at the Harrods Shop owned by the Egyptian born mogul – Alfayad whose son died in the road traffic accident with Princess Diana.

In London, I was declared "Star of Africa" in London – United Kingdom and I had a short term assignment and attachment to Barclays Bank Group Crime Prevention, Fraud Investigations and Anti-Money laundering - Central Operations - Avon House, Westwood Park, Coventry – Ipswich.

The following year 2002, I was nominated and commended by Sir Peter Middleton – Chairman Barclays Bank PLC for the Chairman's Awards for Community and Diversity for the impressive Community Service. I bought my first house through the Bank loan mortgage in 2003 along Khola road in woodlands.

As a Manager responsible for Investigations and Security at the Bank, I reviewed an investigation which had been carried out pertaining to the day-light Bank robbery which occurred at Barclays Bank Ridgeway Priority Banking Centre. This was a view to draw Lessons Learnt and ensure that loopholes identified were sealed and plugged off through a documented game plan and blue print.

As the incident had happened several years before joining Barclays Bank my mind would just wonder as I was not at the scene of the incidence. My mind would just echo and imagine what may have happened but my assignment was critical to save lives of staff and customers, bank assets, reputation and shareholder value.

To catch a thief, I had been trained to think and act as a thief and sometimes behave like one. The Bank robber could have shouted to everyone in that small branch; "Don't move the money belongs to the Bank. Your life belongs to you." Everyone in the bank lied down quietly. All of them were female workers. This is called "Mind Changing Concept" Changing the conventional way of thinking.

When the Branch Manager and member of staff – a beautiful lady I'm told who later migrated to the United

Kingdom after the traumatic experience lay on the table provocatively, the robber must have shouted at her: "Please be civilized, This is a Bank robbery and not a rape case session in a shanty compound!" The Lessons Learnt for me are that "this particular robber was "Being Professional", only focusing on what you are trained to do. To rob and not to rape beautiful Zambian Ladies.

When the bank robbers sped off in an unregistered red Toyota Collora wearing black hoods, sun glasses and went to their hiding place, the younger robber (probably a Private University Graduate – with Masters in Business Administration – (MBA) and unemployed may have told the older robber (who most likely may not even have been in possession of a minimum Grade 12 Secondary School certificate or its equivalent and stayed in Chibolya Shanty Compound). "Bosses - Big brother, let's count how much we got." The older robber may have rebutted and said: "You are very stupid. There is so much unrebased money in those Sacks it will take us a long time to count. Tonight, the Zambia National Broadcasting Corporation (ZNBC) Prime News will tell us how much we robbed from the bank!" This is called "Experience". Nowadays experience may be at times be more important than paper qualifications – especially MBAs manufactured from Matero Compound or Katondo Street in Lusaka.

There is also a possibility that after the robbers had left, the Priority Banking Manager may have told the Branch Operations or Customer Service Manager or supervisor to call the police quickly. But the supervisor said to her; "Wait! Let us take out ZMK30 million from the bank for ourselves and add it to the ZMK70 million that we have previously embezzled and misappropriated from the bank". This may be referred to as "Swimming with the tide". Converting an unfavorable and unfortunate situation to your advantage, not robbing Peter to pay Paul but to pay self illegally.

The Customer Service manager at the Bank may have said, "It would be good if there is a robbery every other two weeks". This is called "Changing priorities and desires". Personal Happiness from unfortunate circumstances where other staff could have been peeing in their pants may be more important than your daily routine job you have been grudgingly performing over the years.

The next day, the ZNBC news could have reported that ZMK120 million was taken from the bank. The robbers counted and counted and counted, but they could only count ZMK20 million. The robbers could have been very angry and complained "We risked our lives and only took unrebased ZMK20 million". The Bank Operations Manager and her co-conspirators could have taken ZMK100million with a snap of her fingers.

The unpleasant lessons learnt here could be that, "It looks like it is always better to be educated than to be a gun brandishing robber in Zambia!" This is called "Knowledge is worth as much as gold!" Knowledge is power even when used in the wrong way.

Together with other Senior Branch Operations and Cash Management team members we, came up with a blue print and immediately recommended and implemented the installation of Access Control systems, panic buttons and CCTV cameras throughout the Branch network and ATMs with reinforced Police Officers and Armed Private Security Guards in order to safe guard Bank Assets, protect Staff and Customers. Line management and Executive members were very supportive of the great initiative and that was the last time we heard of such nasty Bank robbery at Barclays Bank in a long time.

Whilst serving at Barclays Bank, on several occasions, I toured all Towns in which the Bank had branches. It was during the same period when I became Secretary General and later Chairman of the Bankers Association of Zambia – Fraud Prevention and Security Committee.

Chapter Nine

Fraud Audacity - Stealing From FTJ

One interesting case I personally handled was when a Jacob Chiluba of Ndola City – the Provincial Capital of the Copperbelt Province within the Republic of Zambia missaproriated Zambian Millions of Kwacha which were erroneously posted into his account by Bank staff.

The audacity and possibly the novice stupidity of this Ndola based customer and Zambian citizen was that he knew that the money he was abusing, missappropriating belonged to another Jacob Chiluba based in Lusaka. Too bad for Ndola based Jacob that the Jacob's funds he was missapproprieting or "chewing" was the Republican President Dr. Frederick Jacob Titus Chiluba who had gone for 18 months without touching his salary which apparently from Ministry of Finance and National Planning was being misposted to Jacob Chiluba's account domiciled in Ndola.

Having agreed on the approach with the Managing Director and Chief Executive Officer of the Bank then, Mrs. Margaret Dudu Mwanakatwe and other Senior Bank Officials, I had to travel in the night from Lusaka to Ndola.

Relying on the Law Enforcement colleagues and Branch Managers, we raided one bank staff member's home who led us to the suspect's home, apprehended the suspects and had them incarcerated for serious interrogations the following morning.

The remaining assets bought from South Africa and

the paltry funds in his worn-out wallet were recovered. The matter was taken to the courts of law and after testifying in Court as an expert witness, Jacob Chiluba was convicted, sentenced and imprisoned for seven (7) years with hard labour.

I enjoyed working for Barclays Bank as a Senior Manager at the time when Hakainde Hichilema who later became United Party for National Development (UPND) President was the Chairman of the Board, Margaret Mwanakatwe (Nominated Member of Parliament and Honourable Minister under the Patriotic Front (PF) was the Managing Director, Elias Chipimo Junior – National Restoration Party (NAREP) President was the Board member and Chairman of the Audit Committee, Miles Emmanuel Sampa (Hounourable Member of Parliament for Matero Constituency and Honourable Deputy Minister of Ministry of Finance and National Planning – later Ministry of Commerce, Trade and Industry was a Senior Manager under the Treasury Department.

His Lordship William Smith Mweemba - High Court of Zambia Judge was Director of Legal and Company Secretary. Mwendoi Akakandelwa - Member of Parliament and Deputy Minister of Defence under the Movement for Multi-party Democracy (MMD) was Regional Senior Manager for Retail Division. Solomon "Sox" Ngwenya - Focus Capital Finance Ltd MD/CEO was Retail Director. Moses Malunda who later became Cavmont Bank MD and CEO was once the Retail Director. Charity Lumpa who later became MD/CEO for Zambia National Tourism Board, Eco Bank and Airtel was Deputy Director under Credit Risk. Paul Simfukwe who later became MD/CEO for Zambia Postal Service was the Deputy Director Corporate and Institutional Division. Charles Lengalenga who later served as Eastern and Southern African Money Laundering Group (ESAAMLG) Secretary General based in Tanzania and later worked for the United Nations for Somalia Operations based in Kenya was the Head of Security and Investigations at Barclays Bank. David Chewe who later became MD/CEO for Access Bank, Bankers Association of Zambia CEO and Director at ZANACO and NAPSA was the Head of Treasury. Simon Bota who later became the Country General Manager at Multi-Choice Zambia was Head of Projects, Technology, Information and Operations were among the many great team members who served as part of Barclays Bank Central team.

Those were the interesting and memorable days, weeks, months and years. Fine souls and human beings who presented me with an opportunity to learn the Corporate World and some very important lessons in life and my career journey.

Margaret Mwanakatwe during the infamous road shows and Town halls would call all of us "Chaps". This never went well initially by some members of staff who felt like they were senior citizens, responsible married citizens of the Country with children and extended families to look after. Eventually the term "chaps" was grudgingly accepted by everyone within the bank and almost everyone had to use this term to call one another in a jovial and joking manner "Chaps".

Chapter Ten

Fighting Financial Crimes - Zambian Perspective

The great art of combating financial crime risks of money laundering, terrorism financing, fraudulent transactions, bribery and corruption is not for the faint hearted. It must be seen as both a calling and a noble profession.

In a Zambian context, "Financial Institution" can be said to be any legal entity registered by the Patents and Company Registration Agency (PACRA) and licensed and regulated by the Pensions and Insurance Authority (PIA) and, for Commercial, Investment and Retail Banking, by the Central Bank of Zambia (BOZ) which are also among many other Institutions like Securities and Exchange Commission (SEC), the Competition and Anti-Trust Commission are the Financial Regulatory Authorities.

The Banking and Financial Services Act stipulates what a bank operating in Zambia can do. These financial institutions, commercial banks in particular, conduct one or more of the following activities or operations on behalf of customers:

a) Accept deposit of funds, lending, leasing, transfer of money or value.

b) Issue and manage means of payment (credit and debit cards, cheques, International Money Orders (IMOs), drafts, guarantees.

c) Money and currency changing, safe keeping and administration of cash.

d) Trading in money markets instruments, cheques, bonds, treasury bills, foreign exchange transactions (forex), etc.

Financial Institutions (FIs) in Zambia are governed and regulated by laws, regulations and rules which have been put in place by the Zambian government, Regulatory and Legislative bodies, there is no doubt that the challenges facing the banks are considerable and keep on growing.

Externally, the regulatory environment is constantly changing and becoming ever more demanding and intrusive. Whilst internally, as Commercial, Corporate, Wholesale, Consumer, Merchant, Investments and Retail banks within the country expand into more complex products and new markets, all banks without exception are faced with a wide range of risks that must be managed prudently and diligently.

Zambian banks, therefore, should be committed to ensuring full compliance to all local laws and regulations of the land if they are expected to survive longer. All employees, from executives to bank tellers alike, must undertake serious commitments to compliance which should be declared as one of the zero tolerance items that the bank must hold in high priority.

The board and senior management must demonstrate great ability to identify, measure, monitor and control risk in the different functions of the bank. In that spirit, all banks must have a fully dedicated compliance department or function whose role is to ensure regulatory compliance, conduct compliance monitoring activities on a regular basis, as well as provide compliance functions and training to all bank departments and staff.

Banks should not therefore compromise compliance issues in their greater pursuit for more customers and company revenue by growing the balance books and hit the bottom line numbers.

Among the risks compliance teams need to manage are the Anti-Money Laundering (AML), Financial Crime Risk (FCR) and Counter Terrorist Financing (CTF), Anti-Bribery and Corruption (ABC), Trade and Economic Sanctions (TES). The role of professionally skilled, technically qualified and hands-on experienced Financial Crime Compliance and Investigators cannot be over-emphasised. The danger of having trial managers in this area can prove disastrous and costly. The consequences if at all any come along your way are too ghastly to contemplate and complex to handle.

As Zambian nationals may be aware, banks in Zambia face not only banking regulators, but also specialized regulators among which are the Central Bank of Zambia (BOZ), the Anti-Money Laundering Authority (AMLA), the AML Investigations Unit (AMLIU) currently under the auspices of the Drug Enforcement Commission (DEC). Also the Anti-Corruption Commission (ACC) and Zambia Police Service (ZPS) feature prominently.

The relatively latest agency and new entrants on the block is the Financial Intelligence Centre (FIC). Financial Intelligence Centre Act (FICA) No. 46 of 2010 is another great Zambian government initiative and process of establishing additional regulations to create a stronger environment of compliance in Zambia.

The Financial Intelligence Centre became operational on April 1, 2011 via a Statutory Instrument (S.I.) Number 22 of 2011. Through FICA, the Government of the Republic of Zambia (GRZ) hopes to prevent the misuse of public funds, the abuse of the financial system, and emphasize enhanced transparency and protection of the integrity of the financial system. The Zambian Government has attached critical importance to placing a strong oversight mechanism and developing a comprehensive and integrated approach to combat money laundering, terrorism financing and serious financial crimes and all other predicate offences of money laundering.

As professionals in the field of Financial Crime Risk Management and Operations, we ought to take note of the changes under Financial Intelligence Centre Act so that we operate in tandem with the dictates of the Law. We cannot afford to be on the wrong side of the Law as Professionals:

a) Unlike in the past, the Financial Intelligence Centre (FIC) is the sole designated agency for the receipt, requesting, analyzing and disseminating of Suspicious Transaction Reports (STRs) to relevant Law Enforcement Agencies (LEA) and other Regulators.

b) All Suspicious Transactions Reports (STRs) including Suspicious Activity Reports (SARs) will have to be submitted to the Financial Intelligence Centre.

c) This is a slight departure or adjustment in that STRs and SARs are submitted to Financial Intelligence Centre (FIC) instead of Anti-Money Laundering Investigations Unit (AMLIU) at the Drug Enforcement Commission (DEC) as was the case under the Prohibition and Prevention of Money Laundering Act of 2001 (PPMLA). We are yet to know and witness the great benefits of these structural changes which have already been implemented. The Financial Intelligence Centre Act is being revised and amended to fine-tune it further.

d) The definition of reporting entities has been expanded to include among others banks, financial institutions, real estate agents, lawyers, accountants, Engineers and casinos. In other jurisdictions and Countries, this demand has proved to be a challenge to fully implement successfully.

e) Banks and other Reporting entities mentioned in (d) above are expected to report and submit suspicious transactions on suspected and attempted money laundering, financing of terrorism and serious financial crimes. The list of supervisory authorities has been expanded.

f) The Law Enforcement Agencies (LEAs) to which the Financial Intelligence Centre (FIC) disseminate Suspicious Transaction Reports has been expanded to include Zambia Police Service (ZPS), Anti-Corruption Commission (ACC), Zambia Revenue Authority (ZRA), Department of Immigration (DOI), Anti-Money Laundering Investigations Unit (AMLIU) and the Drug Enforcement Commission (DEC).

The Financial Intelligence Centre Act (FICA) has placed some reporting obligations on Reporting Entities such as Banks:

a) Suspicious Transaction Report (STR) must be given to the Financial Intelligence Centre (FIC) if any bank and other reporting entity suspects or has reasonable grounds to suspect that any property was a proceed of crime or related to or linked to crime.

b) The Currency Transaction Reports (CTR) above certain proscribed limits will have to be reported.

The threshold to be advised in due course bearing in mind that Zambia is a cash economy and the currency fluctuates against other major currencies.

c) Banks and other reporting entities are required to ensure policies exist in which said entities are expected to comply with record retention of ten (10) years after termination of a relationship – closing of customer bank account and existing transactions with the banks.

A good compliance relationship with all global and local regulators is fundamental to any bank's success. It is crucial that all banks in Zambia are adequately equipped to fight these risks.

Since most Zambian banks carry out international transactions, all staff needs to be trained and become aware of certain international trends and requirements, as well as organizations such as the Financial Action Task Force (FATF).

Financial Action Task Force (FATF) is an independent, inter-governmental body that develops and promotes policies to protect the global financial system against money laundering and terrorist financing.

Recommendations issued by FATF define criminal justice and regulatory measures that should be implemented to counter these risks. These recommendations also include international co-operation and preventive measures to be taken by financial institutions and other organizations.

Suffice it to say that the FATF Recommendations (40 + 9) are recognized as the global anti-money laundering (AML) and counter-terrorist financing (CFT) standard and bankers need to familiarize themselves with them.

Let us step back a little into history. We all vividly recall the September 9/11. That single day in 2001 changed the world and indeed the life of Compliance, Assurance, and

Conformance, Inspectors and Investigators to name but a few.

In order to further strengthen the Anti-Money Laundering (AML) regulatory framework, Zambian Parliament passed a law known as the "Prohibition and Prevention of Money Laundering Act no. 14 of 2001. In that Act, Part V Section 12, under the Duties of the Supervisory Authority, Subsection 4 states that "A supervisory Authority shall issue such directives as may be approved by the Anti-Money Laundering Unit which may be necessary for the regulated institutions to prevent and detect money laundering." It should be noted that the Supervisory Authority for all banks in Zambia lie with the Central Bank of Zambia.

In Section 13, Duties of Regulated Institutions, Section 1 (c) states that a regulated institution shall comply with any directives issued to it by the supervisory authority with respect to money laundering activities; all commercial banks in Zambia therefore are designated "regulated institutions."

In exercise of the powers contained in Section 12(4) of the Prohibition and Prevention of Money Laundering Act number 14 of 2001, the Central Bank of Zambia (BOZ) issued the Bank of Zambia Anti- Money Laundering Directives in 2004 (BOZ – AML Directives 2004).

Part III of the BOZ AML Directives pertains to Customer Due Diligence (CDD) and other obligations relating to customer identification and verification.

Directors from bank supervision at Bank of Zambia have on several occasions clarified and confirmed that identification of directors, beneficial owners and management of corporate entities is a requirement under section 8(1) and (2) of the said Bank of Zambia directives.

This further clarifies that in terms of management, the banks will acquaint themselves with all key management decision makers in the company. Management would ideally refer to those in top management. For listed companies on the Lusaka Stock Exchange (LUSE) and other equivalent markets like the New York Stock Exchange (NYSE), Johannesburg Stock Exchange (JSE), London Stock Exchange (LSE), information on shareholders is in the public domain and can easily be obtained to assist in the Know Your Customer (KYC) and Customer Due Diligence (CDD) process.

Banks, therefore, need to be in full compliance regarding the identification of directors, beneficial owners and management of private companies seeking to open transaction accounts with banks in Zambia.

In fact, banks should go above and beyond to carry out the unwrapping process of the shareholding structures of certain complex entities. This is actually in line with Bank of Zambia clarification which is very categorical. The Central Bank has confirmed and advised the banks that Anti-Money Laundering (AML) BOZ directives only provided minimum standards.

This implies that the banks should make every effort to obtain additional information that will enhance their knowledge of the clients. The unwrapping process is just one of the many ways the banks should demonstrate their efforts to obtain additional information that enhances their knowledge and understanding of their clients.

Banks in Africa and indeed those in Zambia should emulate the advice of Financial Action Task Force (FATF, along with numerous member countries such as the United Kingdom and United States, which urge risk-based controls.

The Risk Based Approach (RBA) theory assumes that no financial institution can hope to detect all wrong doing by customers, including money laundering and fraudulent transactions. But if an institution develops systems and procedures to detect, monitor and report the riskier customers and transactions, it will increase its chances of staying out of harm's way from criminals and from government sanctions and penalties. This is an area where professionals are needed to manage such risks in such a way.

A risk-based approach requires institutions to have systems and controls that are commensurate with the specific risks of money laundering, terrorist financing and other financial crime. Higher money laundering risks demand stronger controls than warranted by individuals or countries deemed to be of lower risk. However, all categories of risk whether low, medium or high or very high must be mitigated by the application of controls, such as verification of customer identification (passports, National Registration Identity Cards (NRICs), Residential and Physical Address, Utility Bills, Registered Telephone Numbers, ZIP or Postal Code, Know Your Customer (KYC) policies, and so on.

Governments around the world believe that the risk-based approach is preferable to a more prescriptive approach in the area of anti-money laundering and terrorist financing because:

a) It is deemed to be more flexible. Money laundering and terrorist financing risk varies across jurisdictions, customers, products and delivery channels, and over time.

b) It is assumed to be effective. Financial Institutions and companies are better equipped than legislators to effectively assess and mitigate the particular money laundering and terrorist financing risks they face.

c) It is perceived to be more proportionate. Proponents of a risk-based approach claim that it promotes a common sense and intelligent approach to fighting money laundering and terrorist financing rather than a "check the box" approach. For professionals in this field are expected not to be merely ticking boxes.

d) It gives the sense and allows firms to minimize the adverse impact of anti-money laundering procedures on their legitimate customers.

Financial institutions, Banks and Reporting entities need to assure the Central Bank of Zambia, Directorate of Bank Supervision their unflinching support and assurances that banks are fully compliant in terms of on-boarding of individual and Retail, Private Banking, small and medium enterprises (SME), Commercial, Corporate and Institutional customers and clients in as far as Customer Due Diligence (CDD), documentation requirements, identification, verification, record keeping, storage and retrieval are concerned.

The Government of the Republic of Zambia has appointed a new Board of Directors/Commissioners who is expected to give clearer direction and guidance to the Financial Intelligence Centre. In addition the revised or amended Central Bank of Zambia Act as of April 2013 will need to be analysed in greater details and clearly see the impact and implication on the Anti-Money Laundering (AML), Counter Terrorism Financing (CTF), Financial Crime Risks(FCR) and the Anti-Bribery and Corruption (ABC) crusade within the this great Country of Zambia.

It is great to note that Financial Intelligence Centre Act is being amended and aligned in order for it to be in tandem with other equally important pieces of legislation.

Chapter Eleven

The Little Devils and The Enemy Within

The little devils and "the enemy within" are still all out to reap where they did not sow Drain the swamps, don't fight with the alligators. Although the Government of the Republic of Zambia (GRZ), Ministries, Departments, Agencies (MDAs), Parastatals, the newly created Industrial Development Corporations, the Zambia Development Agency (ZDA), State Enterprises Organisations (SOE) and other Institutions like the Zambian Banking Sector would like a situation where fraud and financial crimes could happen to other financial institutions like the Pensions and Insurance, Mining and Retail Sectors, Agricultural and Tourism Sectors, it is an undeniable fact that all Government, commercial and financial sectors in Zambia are potential victims.

Fraud is among the oldest human occupations. Ever since Jacob obtained Isaac's (his father's) blessings by impersonating his brother Esau, the efforts and energies spent by some human beings to get something for nothing has been a recurring theme in literature.

For this Christian Nation of Zambia, those who went to Sunday and Sabbath Schools or have read the Holy Book called the Bible, are reminded that the oldest fraud is told in the Book of Genesis Chapter Twenty Seven (27).

Under modern Zambia and using the current Statutes, Jacob and his mother Rebecca depending on so many factors including political will at the top could have been charged with conspiracy, impersonation with intent to defraud and indeed obtaining blessings by false pretences. Other professional colleagues may also argue that under the current Zambia penal and judicial system the duo would have been acquitted due to unending court gymnastics, adjournments, legal technicalities and political inclinations and alleged political interference.

Fraud is a generic term for behaviour, which involves deception by one party of another. Although the law relating to fraud differs in separate jurisdictions there are common threads, which identify behaviour as fraudulent. These will include the practicing of a deception, the dishonesty of the person practicing the deception, the obtaining of property and/or the intention of interfering with another person's lawful right to deal with property as he wishes.

The number and variety of legal definitions of fraud and like criminal offences are too voluminous to repeat here and those would be covered in other books and professional articles.

Fraud involves deliberate criminal intent and deception. Fraud is any intentional act or omission designed to deceive others, resulting in the victim suffering a loss and/or the perpetrator achieving a gain. Some of the salient elements in Fraud are:

a) Knowing submission of false representation or concealment (knowledge).

b) Specific intent to deceive (deception).

c) Detrimental reliance (losing money or assets).

d) Potential/Damage/loss to the Bank or financial institution or organisation.

Fraud is defined as any loss or attempt to cause loss involving deception. The nature of the deception may include, inter alia: verbal or written statements which are false or misleading in:

a) Applications for personal/corporate credit or current/savings account facilities.

b) Letters of Credit, Bills of Lading or other trade documents.

c) Supporting documents (e.g., audited/management accounts).

d) Internal vouchers or other documentary records such as Local Purchase Orders.

A deception can also involve the deliberate input, alteration or destruction of data on any computer or communication systems and/or involve the use of forged documents. A deception can assist in perpetrating a fraud and also to conceal a fraud or simple negligence.

Some of the practical examples of fraud experienced in Zambia have been broken down Into the following categories:

a) Sheer Theft of cash. Deeping fingers in the till or cash box.

b) Internet Fraud (on customer's accounts).

a) Customer Identity Thefts. Details from the epitaph and tombstones are used to steal pension funds.

b) Card Fraud (credit/Debit/ATM).

c) Loan Application Fraud.

d) Card Merchant Fraud.

e) Funds Transfer Fraud.

f) Lending Fraud.

g) Advance Fee Fraud - Some of these frauds have involved fraudsters persuading innocent victims to part with funds in advance of securing what appear to be attractive jobs or investment opportunities, or loans, which never materialize.

h) Account Fraud - This includes false entries on accounts, fraudulent applications including loan applications and fraudulent instructions.

i) Card Fraud - This includes card skimming, counterfeiting and disputed transactions.

j) Cheque Fraud - This includes counterfeits, alterations, forgeries, raising, cheque- kiting.

k) Trade Fraud - This includes forged, altered or fake trade documents.

The list is not exhaustive and it goes on and on. Fraud involves deliberate criminal deception and is committed by people of all shapes, sizes, heights, hues and from all walks of life.

Pastors, Bishops, Clerks, Ministers and Presidents (of clubs and Associations or for the Republic) have been accused of committing financial crimes such as bribery, corruption, fraud and money laundering.

I wish to submit that just like in corruption cases sheer dishonesty and greed, not necessarily the amount of salary or wages one gets per month counts. When it comes to the question of money, do not trust anyone, and not even yourselves.

This is the reason we can have a very honest and trustworthy Government Office orderly and or messenger but have a greedy, craft and dishonest Church Bishop and Government Minister. In Zambia, we have heard of several high ranking people involved in what my grandmother would only term as embarrassing and shameful activities.

Why would such a situation arise? In white- collar crime, the potential rewards are much greater than in blue collar crime. The risk of detection is lower, successful prosecution is more difficulty as one is able to summon the whole mighty platoon of the best Legal brains in the Country, state counsels and senior Legal men and women to raise preliminary issues in courts of law, apply a dozen of injunctions, a couple of legally challenging objections and adjournments for years on end whilst the loot is diminishing and being shared. The resultant effect is that the penalties are less severe.

What do you expect with "deliberately ill equipped and with no adequate logistical, technological and financial resources" and largely alleged and presumed to be often corrupt Law Enforcement Agencies and Officers who would rather have a drought and poverty stricken but hungry villager who has stolen a cob of maize or a village chicken (free-range chicken) be convicted for five years in prison with hard labour than let the twit swindler of colossal sums of money go scot-free under the pretext of the case being technical.

These are all sound "business" propositions and reasons for fraudsters to put their efforts into fraudulent activities. Those engaged in such criminal activities are many. It is big business and we have seen how unfortunately our society has come to glorify members of the society who have plundered national resources but somehow left off the hook of the long arm of the law. No names mentioned for now.

Loses through fraud in all Government Ministries, Departments and Agencies and financial institutions have increased significantly over the years. There are many changes which have impacted adversely on the socio-economic well being of the Country including:

a) Fluctuation and falling world price of copper which is Zambia's main export.

b) High population growth from less than five million to more than fifteen million within five decades.

c) Unsupported population drift from rural to urban areas putting strain on public utilities.

d) Unplanned mushrooming of squalor and squatter compounds with very few social amnesties.

e) Exponentially rising unemployment levels as more Government and Private Universities and colleges channel out thousands of graduates on the streets with no assurance or promise of jobs insight.

f) Mismanagement, abuse of office, power, authority and corruption in the echelons and corridors of power.

g) High poverty levels (60 to 70%) of Zambian population live below the so called poverty datum line. This datum line is invisible and unknown by many.

h) Steep decline in traditional values/morals leading to all nature of vices. Brothers and sister, wives and husbands killing one another over stolen money.

i) Unexplained failure by Government workers and authorities to make meaningful stand against crime. If there are some, the general populace see those as Empty rhetoric by some Political Leaders.

j) Those failing to be transparent and accountable (according to numerous Auditor General's annual reports) since they are alleged or suspected to be actively taking part in economic plunder themselves.

k) The wrong notion of hero-worshipping and admiration of the fraudsters and the corrupt means used to acquired assets and money through dubious means.

Suffice to state that control systems and framework in various institutions are generally satisfactory, but they are not fool proof against attack from the Little Devils in this Christian nation called Zambia. The "enemy within", members of staff and their outsider ca-hoots and collaborators can actually perpetuate collateral damages to the institutions in which they work.

Those who predominantly perpetrate these types of crime can be profiled among many others in one of the following categories:

a) Intelligent and Inquisitive but misdirected energies for wrong intentions.

b) Too Friendly and charming. Familiarity breeds contempt.

c) Hardworking, very confident and convincingly capable of coning a fisherman to buy fish from a hunter.

d) Too much exaggeration of their perceived achievements in life.

e) Knows the systems and procedures well but for bad intentions.

f) Articulate and may be able to "speak in tongues" to convince unsuspecting victims.

g) Dangerous risk takers and rule breakers.

h) They think they are sophisticated and appear to be wealthy but there is no way to trace their source of wealth.

i) They pose as big spenders, (Zambian musician Mozegator would call them "BIG BUYER" in Social Clubs). If the big buyer support Manchester United Football club, all followers would support "Man U" on that day.

j) Portray an expensive life style and show-off with perishable assets like latest, big smart iPhones, iPads, Samsung, Nokia, LG, Black Berry, posh, big and expensive vehicles which are either obtained through expensive lease or car loans with high interest rates.

k) Aggressive. They seem to be in a hurry all the time. Unlike in Asia, America and Europe, Africans generally don't do things in such a hurry. They love to take their time. They are often late for meetings or wedding parties. Most events rarely start on time.

l) Sense of despair over current 'life experiences' e.g. severe illness in family and genuine financial needs.

m) Name droppers. Smart and wearing expensive perfumes, Brazilian, Indian or Peruvian wigs, designer clothes, branded shoes, wallets and bags.

n) Disgruntled at work and always complaining against life, environment and about everything. They are chief complainants, although they resist resigning.

o) Friendly and charming. Very confident and convincing. They can sell ice blocks and a deep freezer to an Eskimo Headman.

p) Thrive in an office with no segregation of duties.

q) They rarely take vacation or off sick days. Even with a running nose, flu or fever, headache, coughing uncontrollably, they are still on Company desk and stuck on their chairs.

r) They work excessive Over Time, late at night or weekends even when there is no pressure of work or urgent assignments. Constantly working late alone In the office.

s) They make excessive adjusting entries or white-outs in accounting books. Unusual occurrences of mistakes not typical of their professional, personality or character.

t) They Request excessive deadline extensions during monthly closeouts or other accounting cycles.

u) They will usually exhibit a drastic change in life style, throwing parties and drive expensive cars.

v) Will go to great extents to disguise their ill-gotten gains.

w) They refuse promotions, job rotations or changes. Returns to work even on sick leave.

x) Excessive debt, Alcohol or drug abuse; Gambling in casinos, Clubbing, fiesta lounge, Xenon, Chez Ntemba, Lion and Keg, News Cafe, The Times, Rhapsodys, the Latitude 15, Hotels and lodges.

y) Sudden change in lifestyle, behaviour and spending habits. Mostly after establishing unusually close relationship with certain customers giving them special service and undeserved attention.

z) Failed outside business ventures – kantemba, pirated taxis, cross boarder trading (car-boot vending business of shoes, clothes, suites, wigs, Brazilian/Peruvian/Indian 100% human hair)

Third party crime has been perpetrated by various types of fraudsters, ranging from unemployed ex-officials of the Institutions. Armies of these were created by the closure of several major local banks like Meridian, Commerce, Union, African Commercial Bank whose number has swelled by constructive dismissals and downsizing by the remaining Banks, Mining Houses, Government, Ministries, Agencies and other Government wings through so called voluntary separations and resignations to professional gangs and cartels with connections outside the Country.

De-regulation of foreign exchange Controls, abolishing of Special Investigations Team on Economy and Trade (SITET), the liberation of the economy, even with the Balance of Payment (Statutory Instruments number S.I. 33

and S.I. 55 before they were withdrawn have made it possible for criminals to remit fraudulently obtained money, which hitherto had been prevented under the exchange control regulations.

In Government Ministries, Parastatals, Departments and Agencies, including private sectors, Internal and external Auditors, Internal Investigations teams have been able to identify, apprehend and effect a "citizens' arrest" of the culprits in most of the criminal cases.

Whilst some of the demoralised and frustrated Police Officers' action has been lethargic, institutions have had no problem in getting them to the scenes of the crime, often by cajoling, providing transport and lunch allowances. Culprits have been surrendered to the Zambian Law enforcement Agencies, the Director of Prosecutions and his team members and subsequently to the Courts of Law.

However these three arms of Government are increasingly perceived to be failing to inspire the Zambian people, failing to deliver or are painfully slow to reform and administer justice and subsequently fraudsters are left scot-free. Clearly the penal system has not moved with times and the ruling government must assure the general populace that it would not fall into the trap of paying a lip service to resolving the numerous Law Enforcement `Agencies, Director of Public Prosecution Authority and the alleged judicial ills Zambians have been crying over since independence.

Chapter Twelve

Know Your Customers, Know Your Clients

Knowing Your Employees (KYE) is not enough. You must Know Your Customers (KYC) as well. There is no doubt that the challenges facing the Banks and other Financial Institutions are considerable and growing. Externally, the regulatory environment is constantly changing and becoming ever more demanding whilst internally, as Commercial Banks and other Financial Institutions expand into more complex products and new markets, many Banks and other Financial Institutions are faced with a wide range of risks that must be managed and managed prudently and diligently. What with the Regulatory Fines and Penalties in the recent past and some lurking in the dark and not so distant future.

African local Banks, International Banks and other Financial Institutions operating on the African Continent therefore should be committed to ensuring full compliance to all their respective local laws and regulations of the land if they are expected to survive longer. From Board of Directors, Audit Committees, Bank Directors, Chief Executives Officers, Managing Directors, Chief Financial Officers, Executive Directors, Senior management Committee members, Senior Staff, Managers and all employees alike must undertake serious commitments to compliance which should be pronounced as one of the zero tolerance items the Banks and other Financial

Institutions must hold in extremely high priority.

The Board and senior management must (it is a non-negotiable issue) demonstrate great ability to identify, measure, monitor and control risk in the different functions of the bank and other Financial Institutions. In that spirit, all Banks and Financial Institutions must have a semblance of a fully dedicated compliance department or function whose role is to ensure regulatory compliance, conduct compliance monitoring activities on a regular basis as well as provide compliance advisory to all the bank departments and staff. Bank's should not therefore compromise Compliance issues in their greater pursuit for more customers and company revenue by growing the Balance books.

Among the risks these Compliance teams of fully sufficient, skilled, very knowledgeable and dedicated staff need to manage are the Anti-Money Laundering (AML), Financial Crime Risk (FCR) and Counter Terrorist Financing (CTF).

A Good compliance relationship with all Global and respective local regulators is fundamental to any Bank's success. It is crucial that all banks in Africa are adequately and prudently managed in terms of diligent handling of anti-money laundering, counter terrorism financing, bribery and corruption and combating of other financial crime policies, procedures, systems and people responsible.

Since most African Banks carry out international transactions some of which are across African borders, all members of staff need to be trained and become aware of certain international trends, requirements and organizations such as the Financial Action Task Force (FATF).

FATF is an independent inter-governmental body that develops and promotes policies to protect the global financial system against money laundering and terrorist financing. Recommendations issued by the FATF define criminal justice and regulatory measures that should be implemented to counter this problem. These Recommendations also include international co-operation and preventive measures to be taken by financial institutions and other organizations. Suffice to mention that the FATF Recommendations are recognised as the global anti-money laundering (AML) and counter-terrorist financing (CFT) standard. The Continent at large is aware of what those recommendations entail and Bankers need to familiarize themselves with them. The Eastern and Southern African Anti-Money Laundering Group (ESAAMLG) and its counter-part the Inter-Governmental Action Group against Money Laundering in West Africa (GIABA) must continue to play their pivotal roles and intensify sensitisation and training. GIABA is a specialised institution of the Economic Community of West African States responsible for facilitating the adoption and implementation of Anti-Money Laundering (AML) and Counter-Financing of Terrorism (CFT) in West Africa. GIABA is also the FATF Style Regional Body (FSRB) in West Africa and works with states in the region to ensure compliance with international AML/CFT standards. GIABA was established in 2000 and has its headquarters in Dakar, Senegal. GIABA consists of 15 member states.

Banks in Africa should emulate the global advice of the Financial Action Task Force (FATF), along with numerous member countries such as the United Kingdom and United States, which urge risk-based controls. The theory is that no financial institution can hope to detect all wrongdoing by customers, including money laundering. But if an institution develops systems and procedures to detect, monitor and report the riskier customers and transactions, it will increase its chances of staying out of harm's way from criminals and from government sanctions and penalties.

Among other many duties, the Compliance Officer especially the one assigned to deal with AML, CTF, SARS, CDD, Sanction Advisory and FCR matters should the following:

a) Provide assurance to the Country Executive Management Committee that the Bank policies are adequately embedded and the local regulations are complied with.

b) Assist the senior management in ensuring appropriate structure, systems and processes are in place to prevent and mitigate money laundering risk.

c) Monitor the adequacy of, and compliance with, local AML policies by reviewing the relevant key risk indicators, trends and risk issues (both existing and emerging risks), as well as undertaking risk based assessment.

d) Provide support to businesses in complying with the new and changing regulations, as well as the relevant Group policies and procedures.

e) Lead and coordinate Country level initiatives to enhance AML awareness and training.

f) Oversee the in-Country and International transaction monitoring effort meant to detect suspicious activities.

g) Where a centralised Transaction Monitoring Unit (TMU) is in place, oversee the performance of TMU.

h) Where transaction monitoring is undertaken by the respective business units, branches and Relationship Managers under Corporate Banking (dealing with corporate customers and Small and Medium Enterprise (SMEs) or Retail Banking Divisions (dealing with individual customers from high risk areas) and coordinate with various stakeholders to ensure adequacy of such activities.

i) Staff are adequately trained and made aware of the most up to date local legal and regulatory requirements.

j) The Continent requirements are adequately reflected in the procedures and system settings.

k) Appropriate methodologies, management information and approval processes are in place to monitor and manage the level, nature and timeliness of alerts and the resources required to action them.

l) Effective quality assurance processes are in place.

m) Review quality of Suspicious Activity Reports (SARs) and ensure timely submission to the appropriate authorities such as Central Banks and or FIUs.

n) Act as the Bank's single point of contact for inquiries related to SARs or investigations.

o) Maintain a good working relationship with the relevant authorities, regulatory bodies and enforcement agencies such as Central Banks, Financial Intelligence Unit, Police, Anti-Corruption Commission, Drug Enforcement Commission etc.

p) Ensure close working relationships with the Business and clear delineation of duties and responsibilities among various parties.

q) Provide leadership and direction for the in-Continent Anti-Money Laundering (AML) effort.

r) Drive, coordinate and monitor initiatives and actions to ensure the Bank operates in accordance with the relevant laws and regulations, policies and standards, for the prevention of money laundering.

s) Where there are grounds to suspect money laundering activities, make prompt reports of suspicious transactions, or proposed transactions, through the appropriate internal channels.

Members of the public need to be made aware that all banks reserve the right to refuse any transaction where, based on explanations offered by the customer or other information, reasonable grounds exist to suspect that the funds may not be from a legitimate source or are to be used for an illegal activity such as terrorism.

Where a suspicious activity has been identified on the account, banks are required to raise their suspicion with the Law Enforcement Agencies or Financial Intelligence Centers or Units.

Most Anti-Money Laundering Laws and Regulations within Africa stops or bars members of staff within the banks to let customers know that they are suspicious and, under no circumstances, they are not allowed to mention their suspicions to the customer. Tipping-off is a criminal offence in most African Countries and one can be prosecuted. This is one area to handle cautiously as there is a thin line to be drawn between offering good customer service, knowing your customer and understanding their business without unwittingly tipping off. Professional guidance in terms of policy need to be clearly stipulated and widely shared.

Bank Staff will therefore conduct an interim investigation by establishing the purpose of the transaction from the customer. They are expected to use tact in their questioning to avoid customers knowing that they are suspicious. Having considered relevant information and if it is believed that the requirements for a disclosure have been met, the Banks will make a prompt report to the appropriate authorities. It is a legal requirement.

Members of the public and especially prospective customers have been agitated mostly by the line or sort of questions and the design of the application forms, and the amount of information, details and particulars Bankers do ask for from them.

It is advisable to bear with the Bank Officials as they are just complying with the law. It is the necessary evil to ensure that the customers' interests and assets are adequately protected. This is not a case of mistaken identities with the "bad boys".

If one is a Politically Exposed Person (PEP) and this category falls within the High Risk Clients (HRC), and when entering an Enhanced Due Diligence (EDD) relationship the Retail Banker for instance would endeavour to know and accept only those clients whose source of wealth can be reasonably established to be legitimate

Enhanced due diligence requires that further steps are taken to gain assurance that wealth has not been obtained from criminal activity. Banks would not like to take cash and deposit the same on a customer's account when that particular cash is a proceed of a reported criminal act with a screaming newspaper headline such as "Heavily armed and dangerous criminals killed a driver and snatched cash in transit (CIT)" or "Dangerous and armed criminals blew up the ATM with detonators or explosives". Those alleged or suspected to be involved in bribery and corruption may have their account opening applications denied or their existing bank accounts frozen or closed. The Gupta Brothers in South Africa is a case in point.

For genuine customers, the source of wealth will be

obvious for example a monthly salary to be credited to the account and no further corroboration may be required. Where more detailed corroboration is required, client interviews, background checks, and documentary evidence are all valid approaches to corroborate the source of wealth.

There is a wide array of sound practices to corroborate a client's source of wealth. Certainly not sufficient are generic descriptions such as Savings; Investments; Inheritance; Business dealings; Sale of a business, General Dealer.

Additional information must be gathered to demonstrate adequate due diligence has been undertaken. This may include reference to publicly available information, in depth interviewing or collection of documentary information so that Banks are satisfied that they have sufficient information behind the generic description given.

The following are some of the Questions to consider. Not all these questions need to be addressed to the customers, some are discretely obtained:

a) What is the origin of the savings?

b) Are funds to be transferred from another reputable financial institution (e.g. a bank regulated in an equivalent jurisdiction)? If so, this may provide some assurance that wealth was legitimately accumulated.

c) What exactly is the nature of the business?

d) Is the business or individual well known in their area/Country or Continent?

The responses to such enquiries should be adequately documented to demonstrate the level of due diligence undertaken. Examples of documents that may be available to assist in corroborating source of wealth include:-

a) Pay slip or contract letter from employer.

b) Financial returns and Audited accounts.

c) Business plans, Sale deeds, Solicitor's letter

d) Trade agreements or other business documents

e) Property deeds and Sales deeds

f) Will or executor's letter and Rental agreements.

g) Savings certificates and Gratuity certificates.

h) Central Provident Fund letters/certificates.

i) Pension letter or Life insurance maturity certificates.

j) Court judgment papers.

k) Lottery results publications.

The above list is not exhaustive and the need to obtain specific documentary evidence will vary according to the individual circumstances of each client relationship. In many cases, where reliance is on an interview, a memorandum of the interview will be sufficient. Various Bank Policies and Procedures will give guidelines on the specific issue and the modus operandi of execution using specific systems available.

Chapter Thirteen

The Zambia Threshold Project (ZTP)

Security is not found by denying or hiding from the changes. Lasting security comes from being able to thrive and prosper, with your integrity intact, no matter what changes may come. Whatever the change of the day or the moment may be, there is a positive response. Challenge yourself to find that response, and to make every change a change for the better.

I have covered my professional career in another book (my memoires) to be published soon. I will just share some highlights of my third employers after Anti-Corruption Commission and Barclays Bank in this Chapter and leave you to draw some professional lessons from it. One thing for sure is that I have never burnt bridges after crossing them.

Time again had come to move on. In June 2006, I had a job opportunity lurking in the dark. Faced with another emotion battle of labling before my family , wife and three daughters now as we had a new arrival in January 2004. My mother and sisters were around in Lusaka. I knew I had an uphill battle trying to convince the gilrls and ladies it was a reasonable risk taking and good judgment to resign and leave the "permanent and pensionable" job in an internation Financial Institution to settle for yet another two year contract with a developmental organisation. The usual questions were "what next" and "what if" the contract wont be renewed?

These are not ease questions to answer especially if you are the only bread winner within the clan and you have head of the house responsibilities over the innocent souls. Moreover, they were right, I had several personal loans and House loans to settle, including the Leased Personal to Holder (PTH) Mitsubishi Rodeo double cab I had personalised with a private number plate registration mark number "KKK 999" which needed to be paid off or surrendered to Stanbic Bank.

My mind was crowded and I decided to drive from Lusaka to Lilongwe and later to Salima, a town situated along the beautiful shores of Lake Malawi. The shores and nice beaches along Lake Malawi made me to deeply reflect and decide on the way forward. On my way back, I was surprised to find that a newly released Flat "Plasma" screen which was going for ZMK18million in Zambia then for a good brand name was costing ZMK6million equivalent in Malawi. The price for the Music Theatre system was similar. I impulsively bought the same for the home and business use.

My wife and I were already running "Rhudies Restaurant and Take Away" along Cha cha cha road, next to ZESCO Kariba House near the Zambezi River Authority. Upon my arrival in Lusaka, my sisters who had travelled all the way from Mansa and wife were anxiously waiting for me in the Living room to hear what I had decided on the issue of leaving Barclays Bank. I assured them, I was humbly tendering in my polite resignation letter the following day which was a Monday and give them a one months notice.

I started my new phase in life in July 2006 when I worked for USAID funded Zambia Threshold Project (ZTP), by meeting the late Robert "Beto" Brunn the Chief of Party or Programme Director. I was one of the first Zambian nationals to serve on the Management Committee (MANCOM) as an Executive member on this project which drew a lot of nationalities from all Continents for this important project.

The Millennium Challenge Account (MCA) Zambia Threshold Project (ZTP) was a USD24 million agreement between the Government of the Republic of Zambia (GRZ) and United States International Development (USAID), on behalf of the Millennium Challenge Corporation (MCC) through Chemonics International to assist Zambia in rapidly reducing administrative fraudulent activities, corruption and improving effectiveness of fifteen Government of the Republic of Zambia (GRZ) institutions. My two year Contract was drawn by and signed with Chemonics International based in Washington DC. Awkwardly, any disputes to any of the contractual conditions had to be resolved in the USA. Luckily, there were none and we never went that route.

I was responsible for Institutional reforms, capacity building, promoting Sound Economic Governance Transparency and Accountability. Interesting enough, the Anti-Corruption Commission (ACC) my former employers were among the key partners and project funds recipients.

I'm very glad that my resignation a couple of several years earlier was smooth and cordial. I had to face and interact with the same people and former bosses and colleagues I had worked with in my career formative stages. Never burn bridges after crossing them as you will surely need them on your way back or when the lion wants to have a brunch of you, you may use the same bridge to run away and seek refuge.

More eye opening in life was when an African proverb which implores human beings never to undermine or mistreat a fellow human being as you may never know what potential lies in him and Gods plan for such a soul.

Apparently, on the same Zambia threshold Project, as a member of the Executive I had to recommend, interview, decide, determine a pay and work with two of my former superiors. The two were very senior line Managers at

Director level when I was just an Assistant Manager at the Commission.

By the Project design, my former bosses were to start reporting into me. Out of the African courtesy and respect for them, I convinced my Project Director to assign them in the next Department so that we could only be collaborating and working with them instead of working with me and under me.

Of course I had negotiated for a higher pay than them since I was coming from a private sector and since I was poached and enticed to leave my "permanent and pensionable" employment where I was guaranteed to work for the next 17 years before the mandatory retirement age of 55 years then. I call it life and living.

Here I was, serving the Nation in another capacity. Trying to minimize opportunities for corruption and to reduce administrative barriers that stall new business and investor activity and increase efficiency of border operations.

To achieve these objectives, the Zambia Threshold Project aimed at building the capacity of the Government of Zambia's Anti-Corruption Commission to continue leading Government of the Republic of Zambia's efforts to prevent administrative corruption and implement the National Corruption Prevention Plan.

Mr. Nixon Banda was the Director General then and my former immediate line Manager Mrs. Rosewin Mutinta Wandi was the Deputy Director General. We also worked with three government institutions, the Ministry of Lands and Natural Resources, the Immigration Department under Ministry of Home Affairs, and the Zambia Revenue Authority to reduce opportunities for administrative corruption.

Mrs. Ndiyoyi Mutiti who later became Zambia's Ambassador accredited to Zimbabwe and the late Mr. Chriticles Pandeli Mwansa were at the helm of Immigration Department and Zambia Revenue Authority (ZRA) respectively. The project activities included implementing institutionally tailored regulatory and process reform, support the establishment of internal integrity committees, and creating effective citizen monitoring and reporting mechanisms.

The Zambia Threshold Project also played a part in establishing the Zambia Development Agency (ZDA) as an effective one-stop shop for foreign businesses and investors, bringing together the operations of five statutory agencies.

It was the project mandate to reduce red tape to minimize the start-up costs for business investment and licensing, including supporting the expansion of the Patents and Companies Registration Agency (PACRA) into provincial capitals to reduce the cost of doing business outside Lusaka.

Increasing the efficiency and effectiveness of border management operations by building capacity in modern customs and inspections techniques, with Zambia Revenue Authority, (ZRA), the Zambia Bureau of Standards, and Ministry of Agriculture and Co-operatives (MACO's) Plant Quarantine and Phytosanitary Service. Not forgetting the Ministry of Lands and Natural Resources. The project had to rationalize and simplify the economic regulatory framework.

The efforts, challenges and successes of this phase of my life working on this Project have been covered in subsequent books.

Conclusion

The fight against all forms of Financial Crimes is like running a race with no finishing line. As criminals become more sophisticated in their attempts to steal money, value and assets from financial institutions, organizations, pension and revenue authorities, mines and Government Coffers, so must the effort to create better security features and prevention strategies increase thereby slowing financial crime proliferation.

We all need not sit on our laurels and wait for a fraud to occur within our work places and then we start calling on Law enforcement Officers or the Auditor General's Office to investigate and establish what was happening within our sphere of influence. We can avoid the proverbial closure of the pane when the horse has already bolted.

It is a zero option, we just have to painfully realise sooner rather than later that in Africa, punishment of fraudsters and recoveries of stolen funds are so rare that prevention is the only viable course of action. Effective preventative measures are much cheaper and far less painful than post-financial crime investigations and litigations. It is better to drain the swamps than to fight the alligators. The extent of preparedness for this growing challenge to all Africans cannot be overemphasized.

Never stand aloof, whenever you smell a fraud or whenever corruption occur Speak up, speak out, whistle blow, tell the Transparency International. Call Anti-Corruption Commission, Phone the Police Station. Inform your boss. Decline to authorise. Take keen interest in reading the red flags in your staff and customer behaviour, conduct and take appropriate remedial steps to either pre-empt or sanction any untoward actions on the part of staff and fraudsters.

While it may be difficult to prevent all incidences of

financial crimes, it is possible to reduce their impact by performing a fraud risk assessment within Organisations. You should aim to understand the methods of frauds which can be perpetrated by and applicable to each job function. We have lessons learnt from other colleagues and institutions in Africa. They are usually reported in the media both electronic and print media. Learn Lessons and avoid being defrauded.

Let us realize that financial crime is a big industry and there is specialization of labour. Those who specialize in forging of signatures, skimming and cloning Visa Cards, Master Cards, stealing of blank cheques, in impersonating others and masquerading as bonafide customers and known agents.

Fraudsters are busy scheming, planning and submitting project proposals on which institution, which Agency or Ministry with weaker controls they can penetrate and attack.

Fraudsters have needs and wants. Criminals and Fraudsters do plan to celebrate the Birthdays, Weddings, Festive seasons such and Christmas and the New Years in style. They want to throw big and lavish parties. They have a long list of invited guests to attend their wedding or party celebrations.

Fraudsters have Electricity, Water bills, DSTV, Ground rent, Rates, House rentals, school going children and dependants to look after; they have increased school fees for every year which comes. They probably have house construction in Chalala or Mean wood to be completed, a big second hand car to import from Japan.

Fraudsters have to project cash flows and devise means and ways of fund-raising. Fraudsters with misdirected energy and intelligence are smart people who know that Money is in the Road Sector, Construction, Tourism, Agricultural Sector, Revenue Collections and Authority, money is kept in Bank accounts and the Big Banks. They will carefully plan and identify the weakest link among the staff and strike. You obviously do not wish to be the weakest link.

There is no honour in committing fraud. Do not connive and collude with fraudsters, they will dump you and leave you in deep trouble because they can't keep their word. That is their nature. Be alert! Be vigilant! Wake up and speak up! Defend your territories from the yoke of impostors, conmen and conwomen masquerading as bonafide customers and middle men.

All organizations are subject to fraud risks. Large frauds have led to the downfall of entire organizations, massive investment losses, significant legal costs, incarceration of key individuals, and erosion of confidence in capital markets. Publicized fraudulent behaviour by key executives has negatively impacted the reputations, brands, and images of many organizations around the globe.

Reactions to recent Institutional and corporate scandals have led the public and stakeholders to expect organizations to take a "no financial crime tolerance" attitude. Good governance principles demand that an organization's board of directors, or equivalent oversight body, ensure overall high ethical behaviour in the organization, regardless of its status as public, private, government, or not-for-profit, NGOs and NGIs (Non Government Individuals); its relative size; or its industry.

The board's role is critically important because historically most major financial crimes and frauds are perpetrated by senior management in collusion with other employees. Vigilant handling of fraud cases within an organization sends clear signals to the public, stakeholders, and regulators about the board and management's attitude toward fraud risks and about the organization's fraud risk tolerance. What we heard about Zambia Railways Limited was never inspiring.

In addition to the board, personnel at all levels of the organization including every level of management, Chief

Executive Officers, Managing Directors, Executive Management Committee members, Senior staff, internal auditors, as well as the organization's external auditors have responsibility for dealing with financial crime risk. Particularly, they are expected to explain how the organization is responding to heightened regulations, as well as public and stakeholder scrutiny; what form of financial crime risk management program the organization has in place; how it identifies financial crime risks; what it is doing to better prevent financial crime risk, or at least detect it sooner; and what process is in place to investigate financial crime risk and take corrective action.

There are guides designed to help address these tough issues. The same guide recommends ways in which boards, senior management, internal auditors, and financial crime risk preventions/Financial crime risk Management teams, financial crime risk investigators can fight financial crime risk in their organization. Specifically, it provides credible guidance from leading professional organizations that defines principles and theories for financial crime risk management and describes how organizations of various sizes and types can do the same.

Given the alluded to shortcomings, Africans need to take concrete steps to arrest the scourge of Financial crime risks in all sectors of the economy. We need to learn lessons and have a deeper understanding of the concepts and theories or typologies of money laundering, terrorism financing, corruption and various operations of fraudsters so that knowledge acquired can further enhance our capabilities to review systems and controls which are breached and recommend remedial measures resulting in tighter controls being adopted which will subsequently thwart further fraud attempts in many organisations. We need to develop comprehensive and coherent strategies to address various forms of malpractices by all stakeholders.

We strongly believe in mother Africa and the great people of this blessed continent. We are very confident that if managerial accountability and transparency is embodied in the financial sector coupled with good corporate Governance, Ministries, Departments and Agencies, law enforcement, the Prosecuting Authority and Judiciary, the corporate governance of such institutions would be easier thereby reducing criminal activities which inevitably bring about lack of investor confidence, capital flight, closures of companies and industries and consequently create untold misery on the already helpless citizenry who will have little to do apart from engaging themselves in criminal activities.

The key to these measures being effective is the relationship between the banks and other service providers and their clients. A suspicious transaction Report (STR) can only be effective when the bank or indeed any financial institution knows that their respective clients are receiving funds or transmitting funds not in the usual course of business, or in excess of what it makes or receives in the usual course of business. Sometimes it is nature and the type of transactions clients' effect with persons in the banking system will enable the bank to see a strange or unusual pattern in the business dealings. Similarly, an insurance broker whose client only takes out third party insurance should be wary when the same client is now taking out comprehensive insurance on expensive cars, taking out new policies for expensive houses, boats and other assets. These are the unusual patterns that show money laundering at work. How will my bank spot unusual patterns if its records on my bank account aren't enough to alert it to sudden large payments in my account, transfers of money to accounts in the Cayman Islands, Colombia or Pakistan? A civil servant transferring money to Pakistan or Afghanistan? A public service worker receiving USD200,000 cash in her account or keeping large sums of money in the account in excess of salary payments? The Bank must be able to spot the difference between a payment into my account of gratuity and that

STR arising from a deposit or transfer of USD450,000 from a third party such as a Road Contractor. Know Your Customer (KYC) and Customer Due Diligence (CDD) is more than just asking client for details and updates of those details, it's about examining the details, independently confirming they are correct and monitoring them for continued accuracy.

About The Author

Kunda Kalaba is a Zambian private citizen. A professional with 25 years' experience in managing public and private sector Financial Crime Compliance (FCC), Anti-Money Laundering (AML), Counter-Terrorism Financing (CTF), Trade and Economic Sanctions, Anti-Bribery and Corruption (ABC), Customer Due Diligence (CDD), Know Your Customer (KYC), High Risk Clients such as Politically Exposed Persons (PEPs), Jurisdictions and Industries, Suspicious Activity Report Reports (SARs), Cash Transaction Reports (CTRs), Customer Transaction Surveillance, Monitoring and Periodic Reviews, Crime Intelligence Operations, Fraud Prevention and Examination, Fraud Investigations, Security, Law Enforcement Agency and Regulatory Compliance.

Currently serving on the World Advisory Council of the Association of Certified Fraud Examiners (ACFE) Kunda

Kalaba is also a member of the African Task Force Organising Committee, Speaker and Presenter at International Conferences for Association of Certified Anti-Money Laundering Specialists (ACAMS). Member of the Association of Certified Compliance Professionals in Africa (ACCPA). Once served as Chairperson, Anti-Bribery and Anti-Corruption Working Group. He is a founder member of the Institute of Directors (IoD), Zambian Chapter and St, Clement's Old Boys Association. Highly skilled and versatile Certified Fraud Examiner (CFE), Certified Anti-Money Laundering Specialist (CAMS) and Certified Anti-Bribery and Corruption (ABC) professionally qualified with vast and sound experience in Financial Crime Risk Deterrence, Prevention, Detection, Investigations, Security and Prosecutions. He worked in several Countries within Sub-Saharan Africa, Europe, Asia Pacific and Middle East with the Law Enforcement Agency, the Developmental Organisation and three International Banks.